THE TAFT MUSEUM
Its History and Collections

THE
TAFT
MUSEUM

*The History of the Collections
and the Baum-Taft House*

HUDSON HILLS PRESS · NEW YORK

Published in the United States by Hudson Hills Press, Inc., Suite 1308, 230 Fifth Avenue, New York, NY 10001-7704.

Distributed in the United States, its territories and possessions, Canada, Mexico, and Central and South America by National Book Network. Distributed in the United Kingdom and Eire by Art Books International Ltd. Exclusive representation in Asia, Australia, and New Zealand by EM International.

For Hudson Hills Press

Editor and Publisher: Paul Anbinder

Copy Editor: Fronia W. Simpson

Proofreader: Lydia Edwards

Indexer: Karla J. Knight

Designer: Howard I. Gralla

Composition: U.S. Lithograph, typographers

Manufactured in Japan by Dai Nippon Printing Company

For the Taft Museum

Editor: Dr. Edward J. Sullivan

General Editor: Dr. Ruth Krueger Meyer, Director of the Taft Museum 1983–1993

Associate Editor: David Torbet Johnson, Assistant Director / Curator of Collections, Taft Museum

Copy Editor: Catherine L. O'Hara, Publications / Press Officer, Taft Museum

Photographers: Tony Walsh, Cincinnati, Ohio, and Anthony Lauro, Columbus, Ohio

The preparation of the manuscript for this publication was supported in part by:
Two grants from the National Endowment for the Arts, a federal agency;
The Corbett Foundation, Cincinnati, Ohio;
The Getty Grant Program, Santa Monica, California;
The Thomas J. Emery Memorial, Cincinnati, Ohio.

The paperbound edition of this publication was made possible with grants from The Procter & Gamble Fund and the National Endowment for the Humanities, a federal agency.

Library of Congress Cataloguing-in-Publication Data

The Taft Museum : its history and collections
Edward J. Sullivan, Ruth Krueger Meyer.—1st ed.
p.   cm.
Includes bibliographical references and indexes.
Contents: v. 1. Preface—v. 1, A. An introduction to the art collection of Charles Phelps and Anna Sinton Taft—v. 1, B. Introduction to the collection of European and American paintings in the Taft Museum—v. 2, C. European decorative arts at the Taft Museum—v. 2, D. The Taft collection of Chinese porcelains.
ISBN 1-55595-106-6 [v. 1, A].
1. Taft Museum—History. 2. Taft, Charles P. (Charles Phelps), 1843–1929—Art collections—Catalogues. 3. Taft, Anna Sinton, d. 1931—Art collections—Catalogues. 4. Art—Private collections—Ohio—Cincinnati—Catalogues. 5. Taft Museum—Catalogues. I. Sullivan, Edward J. II. Meyer, Ruth Ann Krueger. III. Taft Museum.
N550.5.T34   1994
708.171'78—dc20   94-16313 CIP

Contents

Director's Foreword

WORLD-CLASS ART, monumental architecture, social history, a domestic atmosphere—the variety that is the Taft Museum is reflected in the essays and illustrations that follow. Whether it is the history of domestic architecture and interior design from the Federal period through the 1920s; the story of a philanthropic couple who devoted their lives to art, music, and public education; the history of art from medieval Europe and the great dynasties of China through painting and sculpture of the early twentieth century—each area provides the reader and museum visitor with an exceptional experience that could not be had elsewhere.

This same variety of experience, which makes the Taft Museum a must for visitors to the city as well as a hometown favorite, brought me to the Taft, first as a member of the Taft Museum Committee and now as director. I am delighted that these volumes will permit even more people to share our love of this unique institution and am grateful to the many people who have made them possible.

The preparation of the manuscript for this catalogue was supported in part by two grants from the National Endowment for the Arts, a federal agency, which were matched by grants from the Corbett Foundation, Cincinnati, and the Getty Grant Program, Santa Monica, California. In addition, the Thomas J. Emery Memorial in Cincinnati provided a generous grant in support of color photography of the permanent collections.

During the ten-year period that the Taft Museum's staff has worked to compile this catalogue of the collections, the museum's administrative staff and advisory committee rose to the challenge of raising the necessary funds to publish these books. The hardbound edition has been made possible with generous grants from local philanthropic and corporate foundations, including the Louise Taft Semple Foundation; the Eleanora C.U. Alms Trust, Fifth Third Bank, Trustee; the Greater Cincinnati Foundation; the Robert and Adele Schiff Foundation; and the Ohio Valley Foundation. In addition, the Getty Grant Program, which had previously funded the preparation of the manuscript, continued to support this project by providing a second grant to help offset publication costs.

Members of the extended Taft family were instrumental in securing grants and contributed personally to this project. The management of the Taft Museum and the Cincinnati Institute of Fine Arts acknowledges the generous gifts made by Mr. and Mrs. John T. Lawrence, Jr., Mr. and Mrs. John T. Lawrence III, Mrs. Margo Tytus, Mr. and Mrs. Robert A. Taft II, and Mr. Seth C. Taft.

Two longtime members of the Taft Museum Committee and devoted patrons of the Taft Museum provided much needed advice and funding for this project: Dr. Martin and Dr. Carol M. Macht and Mr. and Mrs. John W. Warrington.

A separate fund-raising campaign was initiated to produce an economically accessible softcover edition of this research for the Cincinnati public. The paperbound edition of this catalogue was made possible with grants from the Procter & Gamble Fund and the National Endowment for the Humanities, a federal agency. We are grateful to both of these supporters for understanding and endorsing our desire to have these books readily available to our local audiences.

Phillip C. Long, DIRECTOR

Preface

FOR SIXTY YEARS the Taft Museum has welcomed its visitors to the display of an international collection of fine arts objects housed in a landmark building. The people of Cincinnati, to whom by its charter the museum was given, as well as regional visitors and travelers from all over the world, have found here the personal collection of a local couple, Anna Sinton and Charles Phelps Taft, whose dedication to public enjoyment of the arts was manifested not only through the museum that bears their name but also through their many other philanthropies.

As the museum approached its sixtieth anniversary, the museum administration recognized the need for a comprehensive publication that would document not only the artistic treasures of the collection but also the motivations of our founders in creating an art museum. We felt that two perspectives on that activity would be required. To that end, we have endeavored to write a history of our museum that both the general audience and the scholar can use. We know that this publication, like all our public programs, must reach out to those in our potential audience who have either not yet visited us or not known of the museum's existence.

This catalogue supersedes a handbook published in the early years of our public history and subsequently reissued with slight revisions. Our goal has been to make a record of new expert opinions, informed by international research standards and presented in a style that our public can enjoy. From the outset we have planned to publish the catalogue in both hard- and paperbound editions. The latter edition is available in four separate volumes that give readers the opportunity to purchase them as their interests dictate. The first volume of this series tells the story of the successive residents of the Baum-Taft House and how it became a museum open to many visitors, even in the Tafts' lifetimes. This volume is followed by three more that focus on the separate fields of the collection—the paintings, the decorative arts, and the Chinese ceramics. Each is introduced by an essay that explains why the Tafts selected these rare and beautiful objects to decorate their home and enrich their lives.

To assist us in telling the story of the Taft Museum, we have selected a team of specialists who could verify the excellent quality of the majority of our holdings. Being truthful, they had also to tell us that certain paintings, porcelains, and pieces of jewelry, for example, must now be acknowledged as deliberate fakes, while others are genuine but only the product of a workshop and not from a master's hand. Glancing over the catalogue entries on every object we learn that the Tafts were, on the whole, fortunate in their purchases and that their mistakes were no greater or more frequent than the errors of judgment made by other collectors of their time (and since). The usefulness of such entries to the contemporary reader is that they may stimulate more careful investigation in personal collecting, while they should encourage the taking of an occasional risk on an unsigned but perfectly convincing work of art.

Furthermore, we asked our catalogue authors to explain to current audiences the significance of our collection within the context of the art-collecting practices of Americans in the first quarter of this century. The Tafts were by no means the only wealthy couple who could buy valuable things and endow public museums through their generosity, nor were they the richest. But occasionally they did make a purchase that earned them the envy of other great collectors.

In preparing this publication, we have also considered the growing public interest in historic preservation of both architecture and interior design. Thus, to the list of specialists in the fields of European old-master paintings, decorative arts, and Chinese ceramics we have added contributions from those who have studied the history of American architecture, furniture, and domestic decoration. The Taft Museum is rare for its combination of features: early-nineteenth-century American domestic architecture; examples of European and American interior furnishings and decoration, including unique mural paintings from the mid-nineteenth century; and the display of a world-famous collection of art works dating from about 1250 to 1906. The thoughtful integration of this ensemble has earned the Taft Museum its international reputation.

The research phase of the preparation of this publication has already prompted us to make many changes in the presentation and interpretation of our collections and our house to attract the new audiences that await us. Reevaluation of two fields, the Chinese porcelains and the European ornamented wares and watches, has led to displays that focus the viewer's attention more on aspects of their manufacture and decoration than was previously the case. The paintings will be reordered in the galleries to highlight some often overlooked masterpieces and to create chronological and stylistic groupings. And gallery renovations already underway are designed to enhance the federal-period atmosphere of the Baum-Taft house.

This publication is therefore more than an accumulation of scholarly detail—the factual matters of attribution and authenticity—although it certainly affirms the regard our professional colleagues have long shown our collections. The Taft Museum has always embodied the wisdom, vision, and capacity for enjoyment of the arts that our founders possessed. Their love of the arts and their further commitment to sharing the collection with the public has become the modern Taft Museum's mission, exemplified by these volumes. More than just a set of books, this catalogue offers us the opportunity to renew our faithfulness to Charles and Anna Taft's commitment to art and its role in public education.

Ruth Krueger Meyer, DIRECTOR

Acknowledgments

Over the course of more than a decade, many friends and colleagues have given unstintingly of their advice and encouragement toward the making of this publication. As in any attempt to express thanks for a project of this magnitude, some names will inadvertently be omitted, but it is hoped that everyone who participated in even the smallest way will feel recompensed by seeing the work accomplished.

For myself, the organization of the publication was done in payment of the debt one owes one's mentor for the inspiration that shapes and guides one's career. Professor Fred Licht, Boston University, was among the first to hear of my appointment as director of the Taft Museum in 1983. During our subsequent phone conversation, we discussed the need for a new catalogue of the museum's collections, and he signed on as editor. Although Licht was later forced to withdraw from his editorial role, his appointed successor, Dr. Edward J. Sullivan, professor of art history at New York University, carried through with dedication and enthusiasm.

Of singular importance to the success of our publication has been the participation of Paul Anbinder, president of Hudson Hills Press, New York. As our publisher, Anbinder endorsed our decision to set the highest standards for the project, and he steadfastly retained and reinforced that commitment. He brought to the publication the sensitive editorial skills of Fronia W. Simpson, whose challenges to our scholars burnished their entries and resolved many issues of documentation.

Through the participation of our team of scholars, the significance of this publication for the museum was greatly magnified. Their visits to Cincinnati for research and public lectures afforded our staff opportunities to examine objects in the collection with them, hear their musings, and thereby profit from their experience. Many of them have since provided consultation on a variety of topics ranging from conservation to exhibitions and interpretation. Collectively, they have helped to reshape our education program and gallery installations.

Several museum colleagues and independent scholars deserve special recognition for their assistance in identifying writers for the European decorative arts. Olga Raggio, chair of the department of European sculpture and decorative arts at the Metropolitan Museum of Art, New York, sagely guided our selection of members of her department to write various entries in this difficult area of connoisseurship. Winthrop Kelly Edy, New York, identified his colleague Jonathan Snellenburg as the appropriate expert for the Taft Museum's collection of watches.

Special praise and gratitude must be expressed for the efforts of the Taft Museum staff and members of the Taft Museum Committee who have been involved in this catalogue. Assistant Director/Curator of Collections David Torbet Johnson seconded the project in every conceivable way, from fund-raising through endless research in support of scholars. He took up recalcitrant objects that would not disclose the secrets of their manufacture and matured his own scholarship in the process. With the death of Anthony Derham, Johnson, working in collaboration with Anthony du Boulay, completed the section of this catalogue devoted to Chinese ceramics and works of art. These tasks were done while Johnson simultaneously served as registrar and participated in every facet of curatorial and administrative work at the museum.

Catherine L. O'Hara joined the museum staff primarily to copyedit the scholars' manuscripts. She has remained as publications editor and press officer and has written essays for other museum publications. O'Hara has been relentless in her determination to deliver a perfect manuscript, and the reader will greatly benefit from her sensitivity and attention to detail. Abby S. Schwartz assisted with the laborious process of searching for and identifying all the photographic illustrations and preparing their captions while meeting her responsibilities as curator of education. Tony Walsh joined the museum's staff as photographer during the preparation of this catalogue. He has photographed with a sensitive eye nearly every object in the collection as well as most installations. Anthony Lauro, Columbus, Ohio, also provided photographs for this catalogue, including the Duncanson murals.

Among the members of the Taft Museum Committee who showed constant concern for the welfare of the catalogue, I must thank Dr. Carol M. Macht, curator emerita of the Cincinnati Art Museum; Anne Lawrence, great-granddaughter of the museum's founders; Phillip C. Long, my successor as director of the Taft Museum; Robert Stautberg, chairman of the committee; and Sallie Wadsworth, secretary/treasurer.

Because this publication is divided into four sections representing the history of the museum and its collections, special recognition must be given to outside readers and other consultants for each field. Section one, *The History of the Collections and the Baum-Taft House,* benefited from consultation with Heather Hallenberg, former curator of education at the Taft Museum; William Seale, Washington, D.C.; Elizabeth Tuttle and Walter Langsam, Cincinnati; Dr. Zane Miller, professor of history at the University of Cincinnati; Kenneth Trapp, curator of crafts and decorative arts, The Oakland Museum, California; Jayne Merkel, New York; and Colin Streeter, New York.

Section two, *European and American Paintings:* Dr. John H. Wilson, curator of paintings and sculpture, Cincinnati Art Museum; Dr. Gabriel Weisberg, department of art history, University of Minnesota, Minneapolis; Dr. Robert L. Herbert, department of art history, Yale University, New Haven, Connecticut; Madeleine Fidell-Beaufort and Robert Hellebranth, Paris; and Dr. Martha Wolff, curator of European painting before 1750, The Art Institute of Chicago.

Section three, *European Decorative Arts:* Yvonne Hackenbroch, London; Dr. James Draper and Clare Le Corbeiller, curators of European sculpture and decorative arts, The Metropolitan Museum of Art; Hugh Tait, keeper, Waddesdon Bequest, British Museum, London; Anna Somers Cocks, editor-in-chief, *Art Papers,* London; Charles Truman, Christie's, London; Madeleine Marcheix, director emerita, Musée Municipal de l'Evêché, Limoges; Véronique Notin, director, Musée Municipal de l'Evêché; Doreen Stoneham, Research Laboratory for Archaeology and the History of Art, Oxford, England; and Otto C. Thieme, curator of costume and textiles, Cincinnati Art Museum.

Section four, *Chinese Ceramics and Works of Art:* Sheila Keppel, Oakland; Dr. Stephen Little, curator, Asian art, Honolulu Academy of Arts; Dr. Julia B. Curtis, Williamsburg, Virginia; Terese Tse Bartholomew, curator of Indian art, Asian Art Museum of San Francisco; Suzanne Valenstein, research curator of Asian art, The Metropolitan Museum of Art; and Ellen Avril, associate curator of Far Eastern art, Cincinnati Art Museum.

Ruth Krueger Meyer

Editor's Introduction

AT A TIME when art exhibitions have taken the form of media events, and great attention is paid to the enormous prices paid for pictures, some scholars and the public often seem to neglect the permanent collections of museums. Among the basic tasks of the art historian are the study, interpretation, and categorization of works of art so that others can carry out further analytical research. Catalogues of the permanent collections of museums are indispensable for both experts and members of the interested general public. For historians to do their work, they must know not only the location of works of art but also such empirical facts as to their size, media, date, and provenance. The bringing together of such material and extending its significance with historical interpretation should result in a catalogue that serves as a point of departure for a broader historical network of ideas.

Now, when the emphasis of art-historical publication appears to be weighted toward the explication of theoretical aspects of art, the essential labor of cataloguing is not given the credit it deserves. The rewards of such projects, however, are obvious. This catalogue of the Taft Museum is the result of over six years of intensive work on the part of thirty authors and additional experts who have served as consultants. Virtually every aspect of the museum is covered in its pages, from the history of the house and the acquisition habits of the Taft family to an examination of the myriad paintings, sculptures, and decorative-arts objects in the collections.

The Taft Museum, one of the outstanding small museums in the United States, possesses a collection that, in many areas, rivals those of the great artistic institutions both in this country and abroad. As with all significant personal collections such as those of Henry Clay Frick, Isabella Stewart Gardner, or Archer Milton Huntington, specific patterns of acquisition have lent a definite personality to the Taft collection. The Tafts, for instance, had a special fondness for Dutch and Flemish old-master paintings, nineteenth-century French landscapes, and Chinese porcelains. Their affection does not mean they neglected other areas. A strength of the Taft Museum is its eclecticism (typical of collections formed by nineteenth- and early-twentieth-century buyers of art), which provides the visitor (and the reader of these volumes) with a wealth of visual material concerning many periods of time, numerous nations, and a wide variety of manifestations of artistic sensibility.

In its earlier years, the Taft Museum benefited from the care and intelligence of Walter Siple, who served as the institution's first director. Under his aegis, an initial catalogue was published in 1939. In 1958 it was updated with information on provenance and exhibitions provided by Katherine Hanna, the museum's second director. This handbook provided a useful guide for visitors to the Taft for many years. In 1983 Ruth Krueger Meyer, the third director, envisioned an ambitious cataloguing project with full scholarly apparatus for every object in the museum. I was honored to be invited to be the editor of this catalogue and have learned a great deal about the collection in the process. But, more importantly, working with the material and consulting with the authors have expanded my understanding of many facets of the history of art. The all-embracing scope of the catalogue will certainly have a similar effect on its readers. We hope that the catalogue, through its wide-ranging discussions of numerous artistic phenomena, will not only serve to deepen the public's knowledge of what is contained within the walls of the Taft Museum but also stimulate thought and curiosity about the very nature of artistic expression.

Edward J. Sullivan
New York University

THE HISTORY
OF THE COLLECTIONS
AND THE
BAUM-TAFT HOUSE

An Introduction to the Art Collection of Charles Phelps and Anna Sinton Taft

Ruth Krueger Meyer

FORMED over a period of twenty-five years, from 1902 to 1927, the Tafts' art collection was assembled during a period that encompassed both the excitement of the presidency of their half-brother, William Howard Taft, and the tumult of World War I. Although this same quarter century saw radically new developments in the visual arts such as fauvism, cubism, and surrealism, such movements were never acknowledged by these Ohio patricians. Instead, Charles Phelps and Anna Sinton Taft were fulfilling a vision of domestic luxury and aesthetic pleasure established well before their time. That this vision was so splendidly realized makes an account of their patronage into a story of American aesthetic culture at the beginning of the twentieth century.

The marriage of Anna Sinton (1852?–1931) and Charles Phelps Taft (1843–1929), which took place on December 4, 1873, united two native Cincinnatians from among the city's most respected families.[1] They began their lives together in the post–Civil War city that had benefited from its status as a border-state boomtown. During the decade of the 1880s the city would grow to commercial and cultural prominence, and during the 1890s the Tafts would become its acknowledged social leaders.

Anna Sinton was the only surviving child of David Sinton and his wife, Jane Ellison Sinton, who had died during her daughter's girlhood. Annie, as she was known to her family and friends, presided over the house on Pike Street that her father had bought from the executors of Nicholas Longworth's estate in 1871. When David Sinton acquired Belmont, as it had been known in Longworth's day, he restored it to its status as a mansion house, confirming his ascension to the city's loftiest plateau of financial success.

An immigrant child, pioneer, self-made man, and ultimately millionaire, David Sinton embodied the legendary achievements of a prosperous nineteenth-century American.[2] Born in Ireland, the three-year-old David arrived in this country with his parents in 1811 and went west with them. After a childhood spent in eastern Ohio he left home while still a teenager to find his fortune. He found employment in various frontier establishments such as hotels, inns, and dry-goods stores before entering the iron industry in his twenties. He was established in Cincinnati by 1847 and prospered during the Civil War, so that by the late 1860s he was an active investor in the city's public utilities and real estate. Over the next three decades Sinton filled the place left vacant in Cincinnati's commercial world when Nicholas Longworth died.

Nicholas Longworth (1782–1863) remains one of Cincinnati's most admired early citizens, recognized for his contributions to the city's early development in commerce, agriculture, real estate, and culture.[3] To establish a home for his family, other members of which were also noted for their civic contributions, in 1829 Longworth bought a newly built "country villa" on Pike Street when a bank foreclosed on the assets of its owner Martin Baum. In his essay "The Baum-Taft House: An Architectural History," Richard C. Cote analyzes the building's history, and in a separate essay Joseph D. Ketner describes its most prominent artistic feature, the suite of landscape murals Longworth commissioned from African-American artist Robert Scott Duncanson.

Longworth was among the city's earliest art patrons, helping to establish its first museums, import works of art from the East, and provide employment and encouragement for the city's resident artists. In addition to Duncanson, Longworth gave support to Hiram Powers, Worthington Whittredge, and Lilly Martin Spencer, among others. Although the extent of his personal collection is not recorded, it is known that he purchased Benjamin West's *Ophelia and Laertes* (Cincinnati Art Museum) in 1828 and hung it in the Music Room of Belmont, thereby inaugurating that room's function as a gallery and forecasting the house's destiny as a museum.[4]

Although David Sinton did not share Longworth's interest in collecting, he was astute enough to know that a successful Cincinnatian should be concerned with cultural matters. Although his only known purchase was a commission to Hiram Powers for portrait busts of himself and his daughter, Sinton, as a founder of the Cincinnati Art Museum, subscribed to its inaugural fund drive. He was one of a group of five leading citizens who signed the museum's articles of incorporation in 1881 but never served as a trustee. His true concerns are perhaps best revealed through his support of the Republican party and his gifts to the YMCA and to the University of Cincinnati, where he established a chair for economics. Following his death in 1900, his daughter and son-in-law, Charles Phelps Taft, would use Sinton's considerable fortune to exercise their philanthropies and artistic tastes as well as to support the political career of Charles's half-brother, William Howard (1857–1930).

What is known of Charles Phelps and Anna Sinton Taft depends to a great extent on the efforts of William Howard. Charles was the oldest son of Alphonso and his first wife, Fanny Phelps Taft. After Fanny's death in 1852 Alphonso married Louise Torrey Taft, who bore him four children, of whom their eldest, William Howard, became the twenty-seventh president of the United States. Among his many notable acts of public and private service, President Taft collected the family's voluminous correspondence and gave it along with his presidential papers to the Library of Congress.[5] In so doing, he was furthering the mandate of his father, who required all his children to write letters and to exchange the family correspondence. Since the private papers of Charles Phelps and Anna Sinton Taft were not otherwise systematically preserved, these letters in Washington and documents in the archives of the Taft Museum are the only records on which to base insights of the personalities and tastes of the museum's founders. From among a selection of the letters exchanged between Charles and the president between 1901 and 1920, one can evaluate the points of view that determined their acquisitions.

Very little is known of Annie's early life and education in Cincinnati. In her 1964 study of the Tafts, *An American Family*, Ishbel Ross states that Annie attended the Mount Auburn Institute for Young Ladies.[6] If this is true, she would have studied in an educationally progressive academy that was later renamed the Thane Miller School.[7] Annie went to Europe with her father before her marriage. There, both had their portraits "taken" by Hiram Powers in 1870 (see 1931.371 and 1931.372, pp. 308 and 309). Powers's early career in Cincinnati had been supported by Nicholas Longworth, who encouraged many Cincinnatians, including Alphonso Taft, to seek out the artist at his studio in Florence. While in Italy the Sintons also visited former Cincinnatian Thomas Buchanan Read, a painter who resided in Rome.

None of the papers from the years before Annie's marriage have been preserved. But once she joined the Taft family, she entered into the vigorous exchange of letters required by Alphonso and encouraged by his second wife, Louise. Still, Annie's participation was limited since she was taking care of her young family and overseeing her father's household. She and Charles had four children: two sons, David and Howard, and two daughters, Louise Taft Semple and Jane Taft Ingalls. Although neither boy was favored with good health,[8] the daughters did much to carry on their parents' philanthropic interests in the later part of the twentieth century.

An image of Annie's vivid personality emerges from the letters written by Taft family members describing the family's activities. Charles's younger half-brothers and his half-sister, Fanny, frequently stayed at Pike Street when their parents, Alphonso and Louise, were absent from the city. During the early 1880s, Alphonso was in Washington serving as the secretary of war, and he later went to Europe on diplomatic missions. When the senior Tafts were in Vienna and Saint Petersburg from 1882 to 1885, William Howard kept them well informed of politics in Ohio and the social life in Cincinnati. This young bachelor found Annie's home a most congenial atmosphere for family companionship and eventually for his courtship of Nellie Herron, who also lived on Pike Street with her parents.[9]

Annie created an active social life that centered on her home and family. As Charles grew more prominent in publishing and politics, the house became a gathering place for distinguished guests to the city. In 1895 she supervised a major redecoration project when Charles was elected an Ohio delegate to the United States House of Representatives, and a political future seemed imminent.

The education, civic career, and personal interests of Charles Phelps Taft are more fully documented than those of his wife thanks to the family papers and his position as the publisher of the *Cincinnati Times-Star*.[10] He was born in 1843 and went to Cincinnati public schools before attending Phillips Exeter Academy at Andover, Massachusetts. From there he went to Yale, from which he was graduated in 1864. He studied law, receiving a master's degree from Columbia University in 1867; he then returned to Cincinnati to begin practice in his father's firm. Shortly thereafter he went abroad for further study of the law and languages. He lived first in Heidelberg, Germany, for a year and a half while completing a doctorate. During this time his letters to his father describe an extensive program of sightseeing in Germany that focused more on scenery and monuments than on paintings and sculpture.

Toward the end of Charles's student years, he was joined by his brother, Peter Rawson Taft (1846–1889). Peter had just been graduated from Yale as the valedictorian of his class and had meant to follow his brother's model, studying first in Germany and then joining Charles in Paris. Although this plan was followed, the two had very different experiences. Charles was a highly disciplined man who accomplished what he set out to do with little hesitation. Family members frequently remarked that he also seemed to be exceedingly lucky. Peter was not so fortunate. While in Europe he suffered from headaches and illnesses and found the mastery of languages difficult. Even so, Peter displayed the greater literary gifts that might have been expected of Charles. Peter's letters describing their travels reward us more generously than do Charles's since they substantiate how eagerly and thoroughly the two men pursued knowledge of the arts and architecture and the cultures that had produced them.[11]

Founding of the Cincinnati Art Museum

When Charles returned to Cincinnati in 1870, he had lived for many months in Heidelberg and Paris and had traveled through France, Italy, England, and Scotland. Resuming legal practice in his father's firm, he pursued his courtship of Annie Sinton. Following their marriage in 1873, Charles continued in the law until 1880, when he and David Sinton acquired controlling interests in two newspapers that were merged to form the *Cincinnati Times-Star*. In this position he was able to promote the diverse cultural, political, and philanthropic projects that he shared with members of his family. He attended state and national Republican conventions, served in the state legislature, and may have wanted a more prominent political position than he achieved with his one brief stint in Washington as a congressman in 1896. But, after that experience, he returned to Cincinnati to watch over the business interests of his father-in-law, whose health was failing. Putting aside his own political aspirations, while supporting William's emerging career in politics, Charles assumed the responsibility of managing Sinton's business affairs and vast holdings in real estate. William Howard Taft had just undertaken his position as the head of the United States commission in the Philippines when Sinton died in August 1900.

Charles wrote to Will (the name used for him by the family) that the months of nursing her dying father had exhausted Annie.[12] They had been unable to leave Cincinnati for any kind of vacation that long summer, and he hoped to persuade her to travel to Europe with him as soon as she had recuperated. As Sinton's only heir, Annie was now the richest woman in Ohio, with an estate estimated at fifteen million dollars. Within the year she deeded to Charles controlling interest in the *Times-Star*, acknowledging his prominent role in developing the paper. Together, they began to plan for the new life they would share as patrons of the arts and education.

A lecture Charles had given on April 5, 1878, indicated the Tafts' interests in the visual arts. The lecture was one of a series sponsored by the Women's Art Museum Association to build support for the organization's crusade to found a city museum. Charles's title was "The South Kensington Museum. What It Is; How It Originated; What It Has Done and Is Now Doing for England and the World; and the Adaptation of Such an Institution to the Needs and Possibilities of This City." Charles introduced his subject by summarizing how the citizens of Cincinnati had progressed in less than a century from

> the rude hut, [to] occupy houses of wood, brick and stone. We have built our manufactories [and] . . . with our railroads completed, we shall be amply provided with all means of transporting our produce and manufactures to the end that all our other investments may also be profitable. . . . [I]t should be the object of our manufacturers and artisans to compel customers to prefer our city because we can produce articles not only of equal quality but of superior taste and artistic decoration.[13]

Taft next described the British governmental system for education and the Department of Science and Arts, the overseers of the South Kensington Museum and Art Schools. Known today as the Victoria and Albert Museum, the institution first served as a repository for many of the exhibits left over from the Crystal Palace exposition of 1851 and other collections of industrial arts, architecture, and books gathered over the course of a decade. From its inception it also housed a training school for industrial arts and design that was at the summit of a national program of art education.

At the time the South Kensington Museum was formed, the governors of both the National Gallery and British Museum had sensed the challenge of a rival institution seeking funds to support new programs that would diminish their resources. Taft described at length how the South Kensington Museum distinguished itself from the older institutions that were devoted, respectively, to paintings and to artifacts of the classical and medieval worlds. In so doing he expounded on the contrasts between a classical education and the system of education in the industrial arts and sciences. The object of the latter system "is to fit a man or woman for any branch of manufacture, and, during the course of study, to enable the student to direct his attention specially to the ornamentation of metals, wood, pottery—in fact, anything that is manufactured."[14]

When he came to discuss the viability of the idea for Cincinnati, Taft stated: "The difficulties, which we are obliged to meet in establishing an industrial art museum with the attendant art instruction, are insignificant, compared with those which England, in 1851, had to encounter."[15] The Cincinnati school systems already encouraged arts instruction in the elementary grades. Taft noted that a school of design was now needed:

> The designer of furniture should know the history of that branch of manufacture; he should be familiar with the church wood-work of the middle ages, the ornaments and inlaid work of the chests of the fifteenth century, the chairs and cabinets of the renaissance, and the wood-carving of Queen Anne's time. The potter should know the struggles, the hardships and at times, the despair of a Palissy, and be familiar with the history and result of his work. Every artisan should derive inspiration from the best works of his handicraft. The Library is a museum for the scholar. The Industrial Art Museum is a library for the handicraftsman.[16]

In his conclusion Taft returned to his theme of the alliance between business and the arts:

> We can furnish to our own people the staple articles of manufacture such as cutlery, calico, and cheap carpets, and have driven out all foreign competition in such articles, while we look entirely to foreign countries, to France, Germany and England for the finer qualities of textile fabrics, pottery and metal work. . . . [I]t is necessary to make another step forward and to build up for ourselves and American art industry in the finer qualities of manufactures. . . . Our people have excelled in inventions and in mechanical science, and are ready to enter upon new art industries. Let them have that art training, and those industrial art specimens and appliances which foreign governments have found necessary to produce the skillful handicraftsman, and it needs no prophetic vision to foretell that at the close of the next twenty-five years, the American will rival the foreign artisan, not only in inventive genius, but in true artistic taste.[17]

Taft's words were prophetic: the Cincinnati Art Museum opened to the public in 1881, and for many years its collections and its programs did follow the pattern of the South Kensington Museum.[18] However, after the turn of the century, the museum began to acquire collections of fine paintings and expanded its mission to display and interpret works to the public. Thanks to the generosity of many donors, the collections came to represent fields beyond the industrial arts that Charles Taft had extolled. During the first decade of the twentieth century, several private collections were being formed in Cincinnati that would eventually enrich the art museum and the community as a whole.[19]

The Beginnings of the Taft Collection

In 1900 Charles and Annie were a middle-aged couple, fifty-seven and "fortyish" respectively, with the education, taste, and wealth to enter into the lively art markets in New York, London, and Paris. Before the death of David Sinton, they had lived comfortably but modestly out of consideration for his habits of mind and stringent conservatism. It is tempting to speculate that they had been planning their collection for many years, since it came together rapidly in the course of a decade. During the ten years following Sinton's death, they made frequent trips to New York and Europe to purchase works of art that would establish them as collectors of the first rank. They sought the advice of dealers and experts who knew what was available and who counseled them on their purchases. Still, it is evident that the Tafts were more than capable of making their own selections and knew what would best suit the atmosphere of their home in Cincinnati.

A survey of the vendors' statements and correspondence in the museum archives yields a list of unsurprising names. Records of transactions with Benjamin and Joseph Duveen, Jacques Seligmann, and Parish-Watson and Company are all to be found. But the name and personality most prominently associated with the collection is that of Charles Frederick Fowles (1867–1915). A native of Herefordshire, England, Fowles came to the United States in 1899 and probably was already employed by the art dealers Arthur Tooth and Company when he met Charles Phelps Taft late in 1901.

Earlier that year Taft had persuaded his wife to travel with him on their first joint European voyage. He shared his eager anticipation of the forthcoming trip with his younger half-brother, William Howard Taft. Charles and Anna Taft, with their daughter Louise, sailed for the Mediterranean on January 31, 1901, going first to Cairo, before moving on to Athens and Constantinople. Charles summarized their tour in his first letter written from Jerusalem to William Howard at his post as governor-general of the Philippines in Manila. From Turkey the Tafts went to Rome for a month and then to Florence, Venice, and Paris.

A letter Charles wrote from Paris on June 10, 1901, has some significance regarding their future collection. After describing the pearl necklace and pendant Annie bought at Tiffany's (she wears them in her portrait by Madrazo: 4.1931, p. 231), Charles continued by describing his forays among the sellers of

> all kinds of bric-a-brac, enamel work, paintings, [and] old furniture of the XVIth century . . . extremely high in value. I think it would amuse you to see your brother rummaging round in these old antiquaries' shops trying to pick up works of art. I got a beautiful carved cabinet of the XVIth century style of the Lyons school [see 1989.4, pp. 552–53]. I have shipped it home without saying anything to Annie about it expecting to surprise her with it when we return. I saw nothing at the Musée de Cluny that compared with it.
>
> . . . The other day I had an opportunity of seeing the collection of Baron Gustave [de] Rothschild at his home. The treasures which he has are wonderful and they are spread around the house in a very pleasant way, and make one think that the owner has bought them for his own enjoyment and not for the purpose of display. His smoking room is filled with all kinds of Limoges enamel paintings [and] small bronze work so that it is cozy and comfortable and attractive.[20]

From Paris the family went on to London and Dublin, where Charles had to leave them to return to his business in Cincinnati. Annie and her daughter toured Ireland before going home later in the fall. Once she was back on Pike Street, Annie directed a redecorating project to prepare the house for the items they had collected abroad.

It does not appear that the Tafts bought any paintings that they considered to be of great significance on this first European trip. Had they done so, Charles might have mentioned the fact in his correspondence, since he knew that William Howard and his wife, Nellie, would have recognized the names of the artists and been interested in the intention to form a collection. The trip seems to have served instead as an opportunity to study the collections of others, to meet dealers, and to hone their perceptions in the great museums and galleries of Europe. Their visit to the baron de Rothschild's Paris home must have inspired them to try to re-create the atmosphere they found there at home on Pike Street in Cincinnati.

Their first major acquisitions took place the following year on two separate trips to New York in April and October. Charles described the second expedition to Will in a letter dated November 6, 1902:

> We spent the latter part of October in New York. . . . While there we invested in pictures and Chinese porcelain: altogether we bought about fifteen or eighteen pictures, from the best artists. We are having a catalogue made out for them together with a photograph of each picture. I will send you one when it is done.
>
> In the collection, we have a Meissonier, a Gainsborough, a Corot, a Constable, a Troyon, a Diaz, a Vibert and several others. After studying pictures for some little time and visiting the Metropolitan Museum in New York frequently, I have been educating myself in the matter and have come to the conclusion that our collection in Eden Park is a very inferior one. . . . We bought the pictures from Arthur Tooth & Sons who have establishments in Paris, London and New York. They sent a man out with the pictures last week and he has been engaged three or four days in hanging them. The large music room is quite transformed by them. We expect to have electric lights arranged in the ceiling so as to throw light upon the walls for the pictures through prisms so as to equalize it. The problem of lighting pictures is quite a serious one. Annie docs not want to destroy the beauty of the music room by dropping lights from the ceiling. I hope the prismatic arrangement will be satisfactory.[21]

The 1902 catalogue offers evidence that the characteristics of the paintings collection were already beginning to emerge, and the consultative services of Charles Frederick Fowles have been acknowledged. It was Fowles who made the trip to Cincinnati with the first paintings, and this visit inaugurated a number of similar trips during which Taft and Fowles would debate the installation of new purchases. Fowles is also identified as the compiler of the catalogue, conspicuously labeled "under revision" and published by the firm of Arthur Tooth and Sons.[22]

More than half of the thirty works listed in the 1902 catalogue were pastoral landscapes, with the masters of the Barbizon group and their pupils well represented. The fourteen other paintings included two scenes of Venice, two oriental subjects, two portraits, and one marine. There were also seven paintings of that distinctly late-nineteenth-century genre that commented with gentle humor on the lives of peasants and members of religious orders. Such artists as the Englishmen Thomas Gainsborough and John Constable and the Frenchmen Constant Troyon, Jules Dupré, and Félix Ziem were represented by modest paintings that were eventually exchanged for larger canvases.[23] Only seven of these first paintings remained in the collection when its ownership was transferred to the Taft Museum by the Tafts' deed of gift executed in 1927.[24]

During the same 1902 excursions to New York that inaugurated the paintings collection, the Tafts began to buy Chinese porcelains and European decorative arts. In six separate purchases that year from the Duveen firm, they acquired a total of seventy-two ceramic objects, including Kangxi-period plates, vases, bowls, bottles, and teapots. During the next two years this pace of acquisition was continued; twenty-six objects were added in 1903, and nineteen more in 1904.

Although Duveen had initially directed Taft's attention to famille verte as well as blue-and-white export ceramics, in 1905 Taft enlarged his interests by buying a group of forty-nine Qing dynasty monochromes from Thomas B. Clarke of New York. In his one recorded visit to this gallery Taft selected a wide range of shapes and glazes, including those objects originally used on a scholar's desk, such as nine peach-bloom and five celadon water coupes, vases, and boxes; a magnificent *langyao*, or oxblood, bottle vase (see 1931.103, p. 607); and two small porcelain bottle vases incised with *anhua* dragons under a clear glaze and marked with the Kangxi emperor's imperial reign mark (see 1931.119 and 1931.121, p. 612). Taft commissioned the first publication of his porcelains at this time, declaring his interest to become a recognized collector in this field.[25]

Neither the museum's records nor the Tafts' correspondence documents in detail the growth and objectives of the decorative-arts collection, which would eventually number 228 objects. Yet this field of collecting appears no less important to their plan, and it also traces its origins to 1902 when the Tafts first acquired tapestries and two Limoges ewers.[26] With their last recorded purchases in 1924 from Duveen of the ivory *Virgin and Child* from the Abbey Church of Saint-Denis (see 1931.319, pp. 462–64) and fourteen examples of maiolica, the Tafts had assembled a stunning array of *objets de vertu* that included forty-nine European sixteenth-through eighteenth-century watches, ninety-seven Limoges painted enamels, terra-cotta reliefs of the style of the della Robbia school,[27] sweetmeat boxes, rock crystals, pendant jewels, and a Saint-Porchaire saltcellar (see 1931.224, pp. 514–15).

Once the Tafts had begun to build their collection with the assistance of Charles Fowles, they must have sought the dealer's advice on the selection of an artist to paint their formal portraits. Fowles recommended the Spaniard Raimundo de Madrazo, who had been working in the United States since 1901, and arranged for the artist and his wife to journey to Cincinnati for the sittings.[28] Their visit in December 1902 yielded other benefits to the Tafts, who subsequently acquired from Scott and Fowles the painting *An Arab Guard* (see 1931.430, p. 229) by Mariano Fortuny, an uncle of Madrazo. Eight years later the Tafts returned the visit by journeying to Madrid, where Madrazo guided them through the Prado and arranged a visit to the collection of the duke of Alba.[29]

It was important to Charles Taft to keep his brother, far away at his post in the Philippines, informed on the development of his collection. In a letter to Will dated December 8, 1902, he wrote:

> We are still getting pictures and Chinese Porcelain. The most difficult thing to arrange about the pictures is the light; we have finally come to the plan of putting reflectors hanging from the ceiling at either end of the large music room. The pictures cover the walls at either end. They are of the finest quality. Annie takes great pleasure in them and will enjoy them more and more everyday. Last week, she spent most of her time sitting for Madrazzo [sic] the portrait painter. I think she is going to have a beautiful picture. I expect to go through the same operation this week [see 3.1931, p. 230]. Madrazzo [sic] is an artist who has painted many portraits in New York

and has a great reputation. His father and gran-father [*sic*] were artists before him, and painted the portraits of the Royal Families in Madrid. I think that he has caught Annie's expression very well. Up to the present time, however, he has only tried the face, the balance of the picture he will have to fill in.[30]

On the day after Christmas 1902, Charles wrote to Will that their sittings were over. It had taken the painter about three weeks to do the work, and in that time the inquisitive Charles had become well acquainted with Madrazo's wife, a Venezuelan who spoke English and "ran the portrait business" for her husband. Charles thought that their portraits were "excellent" but was having difficulty finding a place to hang them. He had spent Christmas Day having a great time among his treasures: "It is difficult to get me out of the house when I once get settled down at the pictures and porcelains."[31]

The letters Will wrote to Charles from the Philippines were generally intended for circulation to his mother, three other brothers, and his sister. Will usually measured out his personal comments carefully, but on January 26, 1903, he gave a lengthy acknowledgment of the Charles Tafts' new avocation: "We are very much interested in your purchases of pictures and congratulate you and Annie on your wisdom in accumulating works of art. I observe that you stick to the old place with a cat-like love for the situation, but I think you will ultimately have to surrender and move out to the country. Especially is this the case when you begin to accumulate works of art. You must have light and clear light."[32]

Charles sent Will the 1902 paintings catalogue on February 11, 1903. It represented a year-long effort and a major expenditure of funds, but as Charles put it, "Annie and I have about made up our minds that it would be just as well to invest money in pictures as to pile it up in bonds and real estate. At all events, we get a good deal of pleasure out of pictures."[33] Part of that pleasure was to be found in sharing the experience with others. In that same month, the Tafts opened their home to the Cincinnati Art Club on a Sunday afternoon, inaugurating a practice of receiving visitors to their collection that they would continue for the rest of their lives.

In April, Annie, Charles, and their daughter Louise were back in New York on a shopping trip. Charles was looking forward to going to the Metropolitan Museum with Duveen to see the porcelains. And although he does not say so in the letter quoted below, Charles probably planned a visit to Charles Fowles, who at some time during the previous year had left Arthur Tooth and formed a partnership with Stevenson Scott.[34] Writing to Will in a letter dated April 18, Charles Taft said:

> I have secured several additional pictures since I sent you [the] catalogue. We have a beautiful Rousseau; also a Sir Joshua Reynolds, a Lhermitte and Jacob Maris. I think you would not know the old house now with all the new paintings. I expect to have next fall a catalogue made of the porcelains. Duveen promises to get the services of the man who wrote up the Garland collection in the Metropolitan Museum. I expect to have the porcelains catalogued and put in a catalogue, just as I did the paintings.[35]

The "Duveen" to whom Charles refers is probably Benjamin Duveen, the brother of the more famous and flamboyant Sir Joseph Duveen, who built the collections of many wealthy Americans.[36] The catalogue of porcelains was written by John Getz and published in 1904. It contains eighty-three entries, reflecting the extent of the collection at the time. Over the years the Tafts continued to add to their porcelain collection, and, until 1915, they bought these objects primarily from the Duveen firm. Few porcelains were purchased between 1915 and 1920, at which point they resumed collecting and made their purchases from both Duveen Brothers and the Parish-Watson firm.[37] Throughout this period some porcelains were returned and new examples added, bringing the final total of objects in this field to 216.

The great Duveen himself made a trip to Cincinnati in January 1908 for an on-site inspection and wrote his hosts an enthusiastic endorsement of what he saw.[38] Although the Duveens tried to tempt Charles with their pictures, the Tafts were loyal to Scott and Fowles, who seemed to have been more sensitive to their clients' tastes. The Duveens tried to steer the Tafts in the direction of Italy by offering, among other treasures, a marble relief from the studio of the Florentine sculptor Rosselino.[39] When this sculpture was refused, a fifteenth-century painting once attributed by the famous German art historian Willem von Bode to Botticelli was shipped by the Duveens to Cincinnati for approval; it, too, was rejected once Von Bode wrote to Taft saying he had changed his mind.[40]

During the summer of 1903, Charles, Annie, and their children made their second trip to Europe. This time their purpose was to expand and improve their collection. Charles wrote to Will from London on July 12:

> I have been devoting my time to the museums and picture galleries. We have secured two new paintings — a Troyon, in place of the one which we had and a Millet. They are very important specimens. The one by Millet called Maternity is one of the most impressive pictures I ever saw [see 1931.448, p. 265]. They cost a good bit of money but they are of the finest quality and are worth it. They came from private collections. Mr. Fowles, who is specially interested in our pictures was particularly zealous in finding and securing them for us. He has several clients who want a Millet, but he promised me the first chance. As I am on the ground and put up the money I got the chance.[41]

From London the Tafts went to France for seven days of "automobiling" and sightseeing in the châteaux country of the Touraine. In Paris Charles secured a beautiful selection of Limoges enamels:

> [I]t belonged to the same Count from whom I bought the snuff boxes. [The dealer] Seligmann says that this Count has an income of about $30,000 a year and lives at the rate of $50,000 a year, so that every now and then he is obliged to sell off something to pay up the deficit. That is the way in which I happen[ed] to get the Limoges. Annie was particularly pleased with it. I also secured from him a beautiful rock crystal piece. We also bought from another source a beautiful specimen of Luca della Robbia.[42]

During the month of August, the Tafts continued their continental tour by visiting Germany and Holland and passing through Brussels on their way back to Paris. From the French capital on September 2, 1903, Charles wrote to Will describing their itinerary. In Amsterdam they had sought out private collections as well as museums and had made a trip to Haarlem to study Frans Hals, an artist who would soon figure prominently in their collection.

Back in Cincinnati Charles wrote on October 19 to describe their dismay at finding their house in the middle of a construction zone. The American Book Building was going up on the old Larz Anderson property to the south of them. Moreover, the land to the north of the house had been bought by commercial developers, so the house would be increasingly isolated in a business district. Still, Charles wrote to Will, "Annie and I concluded we will stick by the old place," a decision that would be tested several times during the next decade.[43]

After the first of the year more paintings arrived, and Charles continued to keep Will informed of the growth of their collection. In March 1904, they hung a new Corot landscape, *Le Soir: La Fête du Pan* (*Evening: The Festival of Pan;* see 1931.449, p. 247), as well as paintings by Gainsborough and Ziem.[44] Charles noted, "Our great difficulty is to find a suitable place for the Corot. We have tried it in the large room at either end, but it detracts so much from the surrounding pictures that we concluded to put it in the room where the Millet is, over the mantelpiece taking down the large mirror. While this is not a good place on account of the reflection from the windows it still is the best we could find."[45] All the Tafts' paintings were hung behind glass to protect them from the air pollution in Cincinnati. The details of the Corot painting would have been rendered nearly invisible by glare and reflections while the strength of its composition would indeed have overpowered smaller-scale paintings.

In the fall of 1904, the Tafts were again in New York looking at pictures.[46] Fowles had brought over a painting from England with which he hoped to tempt his clients, and Seligmann also had works to show them. Fowles was probably offering the impressive double portrait of *Mrs. John Weyland and Her Son John* by Sir Joshua Reynolds (see 1931.491, p. 184).

Also in the fall of 1904, William Howard Taft was made a member of the cabinet of President Theodore Roosevelt, serving as his secretary of war. After the new year, he settled his family in Washington. The frequent correspondence between the two brothers continued even though they were now able not only to see one another in Washington, Cincinnati, and elsewhere but also to call each other on the telephone. Secretary Taft encouraged Charles and Annie to think about moving to the nation's capital. He knew that Annie would love the social life and that Charles had a lingering desire for public service that might be furthered if he were nearer the White House. Will also thought that they could continue their art collecting in the more amenable environment of a house built for that purpose and away from the soot-laden air of Cincinnati. He had even found a suitable lot for sale on Connecticut and Florida avenues. He wrote twice to Charles about his idea, and Charles considered it carefully in a letter of May 4, 1905, before rejecting the proposition: "I think it would be rather foolish now to make such an important change."[47]

During the next three years, the collection grew in both numbers and quality. Purchases were usually made in the spring and fall of the year when Charles went to New York for business meetings and could visit Scott and Fowles and the other dealers. Fowles had made several trips to Cincinnati in 1904 and knew his clients' requirements and their tastes.[48] Among the significant purchases of 1905 was a group of canvases by Hague School artists of the late nineteenth century; the *Portrait of an Italian Noblewoman,* formerly attributed to Van Dyck (see 1931.447, p. 177);[49] and *The Trout Stream* by J. M. W. Turner (see 1931.459, p. 197). Six Turner watercolors were also purchased, bringing to nine the number of works by this artist in the collection.

In the following year, 1906, the Tafts acquired two major works by seventeenth-century Dutch masters: *Portrait of a Man* by Frans Hals (see 1931.450, p. 141) and *Farmland with a Pond and Trees* by Meyndert Hobbema (see 1931.407, p. 106). Two more great pictures were added in 1907: Turner's *Europa and the Bull* (see 1931.442, p. 199) and Gainsborough's *Portrait of Edward and William Tomkinson* (see 1931.412, p. 182). The striking emphasis on portraiture and landscape was supported by other significant if smaller-sized paintings, including Gainsborough's *Maria Walpole* (see 1931.406, p. 181); Henry Raeburn's portraits of Edward Satchwell Fraser (see 1931.425, p. 195) and Jane Fraser Tytler (see 1931.424, p. 195); two Venetian scenes by Félix Ziem (see 1931.419 and 1931.418, pp. 240 and 241); and two Daubigny landscapes, *River Scene: The Ferryboat at Bonnières* (see 1931.463, p. 267) and *Evening on the Oise* (see 1931.462, p. 269).

The preference for landscapes and portraits over narrative and history paintings can be attributed equally to the Tafts' own tastes and to their commitment to education in the arts. There is considerable evidence that they always intended to share the collection with art amateurs and students. One may conclude, therefore, that their purpose was to provide the best examples of those genres in which an artist of their own time had to excel to pursue a successful career and participate in the contemporary artistic community. Remembering the value Charles Phelps Taft placed on the instructive nature of works of art in his lecture of 1878, the thrust of their collecting program becomes increasingly evident. An American artist of the early twentieth century would probably have a career based primarily on commissioned portraits and the production of popular landscape scenes.

Paintings of religious subjects were conspicuously absent from the Tafts' program. As American Protestants, they would have had little familiarity with the powerful religious imagery of Roman Catholicism except what they saw on their travels. Moreover, they lived at a time when religious subjects were most frequently stated through covert visual metaphors or treated as genre subjects.[50] Traditional religious imagery is, however, well represented in the collection in the examples of Limoges enamels, the relief sculptures, the Franco-Flemish tapestry depicting the Adoration of the Magi (1931.332, p. 547), and the great final purchase for the collection, the Gothic ivory *Virgin and Child* from the Abbey Church of Saint-Denis.

Within this period, art matters receded in favor of political affairs in the communications between the two Taft brothers. By 1908 Charles would have had little time to work with the collection since he was engaged in masterminding his brother's campaign for the presidency. The nomination was clinched in Chicago in June, and the notification ceremonies were held late in July 1908 at the Pike Street house. Charles himself was caught up in the political ferment of Ohio and tried to run for the senate seat held by Joseph B. Foraker, but withdrew when his candidacy was seen to be hurting the party.[51]

Following the inauguration in 1909, Charles and Annie commissioned the portrait of William Howard Taft that was painted in the White House by the Spaniard Joaquín Sorolla y Bastida (see 2.1931, p. 232). The painting was brought to Cincinnati in May of that year, and Charles pronounced it a "success," even though its arrival raised anew the difficulty of hanging pictures in the rooms of the house on Pike Street. Charles told Will, "We have not yet found a place for it. It needs distance and good light. . . . It now occupies one end of the spare bedroom, in a tolerably fair light, but not hung high enough."[52]

The Making of a Public Collection

The problems of displaying their increasingly magnificent collection inevitably led the Tafts to contemplate building their own art gallery. The *Cincinnati Magazine* reported in its September 1909 issue that Mrs. Charles P. Taft had purchased a large plot of land at the southwest corner of Fourth and Pike streets for that purpose. Three new portraits had been purchased within the year: *Portrait of a Man Rising from His Chair* by Rembrandt (see 1931.409, p. 153) and the pendant paintings by Frans Hals, *Portrait of a Seated Man Holding a Hat* and *Portrait of a Seated Woman Holding a Fan* (see 1931.451 and 1931.455, p. 143). The magazine story further related: "It is understood that when the paintings are installed in their new home arrangements are to be made whereby the public will be admitted to view them at stated hours."[53]

The Tafts had already decided to show their collection to a wider audience. Eleven of their paintings were sent to New York in the fall of 1909 for the opening of Scott and Fowles's new gallery on Fifth Avenue. Savoring the experience, Charles wrote to Will on November 15, "They made quite a sensation in the New York art world [since] the two Franz Hals which we showed have never been seen before, even by dealers." A number of their paintings were lent again in 1914 for a similar exhibition at Scott and Fowles.[54] The collection was shown to the public in Cincinnati at an exhibition at the Cincinnati Art Museum in 1911.[55]

After only a decade the Tafts had clearly established the criteria that would guide the development of the collection. The major fields of specialization would be paintings, porcelains, and decorative arts with an emphasis in this last area on Limoges enamels. The paintings collection would feature portraits and landscapes from the schools that had substantially influenced the modern development of these genres: seventeenth-century Holland, eighteenth-century England, and nineteenth-century France, Holland, and Spain.

The additions to the collection made after 1914 must represent the Tafts' desire to refine and supplement previously established stylistic groupings. So, to the eight watercolors and two oils by J. M. W. Turner there was added a ninth watercolor, *Lake of Thun* (see 1931.390, p. 210). A third oil painting, purchased in 1910, *Old London Bridge* (see 1931.444, p. 200), is no longer accepted as a work by Turner. A similar misfortune of deattribution has befallen the Tafts' choice of a view of *Landscape with Canal* (see 1931.467, p. 214), which although graced by the artist's signature can no longer be identified as a work by John Constable.[56] Happily, the Tafts fared better when it came time to supplement their collection of portraits by Gainsborough with a landscape purchased in 1923 and a river scene by Richard Parkes Bonington acquired in 1924 (see 1931.445 and 1931.443, pp. 180 and 215).

During the last decade of their collecting activities the Tafts also enriched their holdings in seventeenth-century Dutch genre painting, which had consisted of works by Jan Steen and Adriaen van Ostade, by the addition of *The Sleeping Soldier* by Gerard ter Borch (see 1931.398, p. 170) and *A Woman with a Cittern and a Singing Couple at a Table* by Pieter de Hooch (see 1931.395, p. 175). Also within this time they purchased two portraits attributed to Goya: one, a half-length portrait of Queen María Luisa of Spain (see 1931.446, p. 223), and the other of the bullfighter Pedro Joaquín Rodríguez "Costillares" (see 1931.393, p. 226). Neither attribution can still be supported, although the fine quality of both is generally acknowledged. However, the Tafts' discerning choice of an early portrait by the nineteenth-century French master J.-A.-D. Ingres, *Mademoiselle Jeanne Gonin* (see 1931.414, p. 235), has never been questioned.

The concentration on European painters in the formation of the Taft Museum collection has long been remarked as deliberate. Of American artists, only Frank Duveneck and Henry Farny, two Cincinnati artists of major reputation, are represented along with the lesser-known John White Alexander and Frederick van Vliet Baker. To this group, the Anglo-American John Singer Sargent's portrait of Robert Louis Stevenson (see 1931.472, p. 295), bought in 1922, was a major addition. Yet the randomness of this selection of works seems to indicate no clear interest in the development of American painting. In the absence of any documentation of the Tafts' views on the matter, the choices must give witness to the supposition.

In the field of European decorative arts, an estimation of the Tafts' program of collecting is to be determined even more by mute evidence. Only three purchases, albeit great ones, are documented after 1910. Between 1923 and 1924 Duveen supplied a Saint-Porchaire saltcellar, the ivory Virgin, and a collection of twelve maiolica plates and two ewers that had belonged to Baron Adolphe de Rothschild. In addition to the late-thirteenth-century ivory statuette, the Tafts acquired only two other significant pieces of sculpture. In 1905 Jacques Seligmann had sold the Tafts a honestone relief depicting the Annunciation by the sixteenth-century German artist Loy Hering (see 1931.318, p. 469). The Virgin and the *Annunciation* are allied in taste with the Gothic tapestry of the Adoration of the Magi and the selection of Limoges enamels with religious subjects.

The third important work of sculpture in the collection is neither religious nor of European provenance. It is a work by the twentieth-century American sculptor George Grey Barnard and probably entered the collection as a gift from the artist in gratitude for the commission from the Tafts for a colossal statue of Abraham Lincoln, which they donated to the city of Cincinnati. Since there is no record of a sale, Barnard must have offered them the marble carving *Solitude (Adam and Eve)* (see 1931.373, p. 311), which has been identified as a study for his larger work, *Urn of Life* (ca. 1895–98 and 1918, Pittsburgh, Carnegie Museum of Art).

Barnard's commission for the Cincinnati *Lincoln* is remarkable for being the only instance of Charles Phelps Taft's direct involvement in artistic politics. No stranger to the smoke-filled room, Taft quite unexpectedly found himself implicated in what became an international incident that eventually threatened even the reputation of his brother, the former president and subsequent chief justice of the Supreme Court of the United States. In an otherwise typical letter to William Howard Taft, at the White House, dated December 9, 1910, Charles disclosed the seeds of the disagreement:

> I am having an annoying time here about the Alms Lincoln Memorial. Harry Probasco is on our committee for the selection of a sculptor. Rabbi Grossman, Will Taylor, A. O. Elzner and myself are the other members of the committee. We all have agreed upon Barnard as the sculptor. Now, Probasco is kicking and refuses to come in. Mrs. Alms constituted us her agents and trustees to carry th[r]ough this project, and we four have signed an agreement with Barnard. Probasco has been poisoning Mrs. Alms' mind against Barnard hoping to push in [Gutson] Borglum, the man who made the Sheridan statue in Washington. He is relying upon a technicality of the law which requires, in this kind of agency, the unanimous consent of the agents. No one thought of that kind of point at all, for we all have been acting as if it took simply a majority of the committee to decide. We four have just received letters from Probasco, saying that he did not recognize this pretended contract and that Mrs. Alms sided with him and that he would fight any effort to continue the work with Barnard; also that Mrs. Alms would not hold herself responsible for any contract made with Barnard. I have been so mad today that I have not been able to do anything. Tomorrow, we will have a meeting; it is our present purpose to draw up a statement, showing the course of the negotiations. I think by the time it is finished and published the situation of Mr. Borglum, Mrs. Alms and Mr. Probasco before the reading public will be rather peculiar. If ever a confidence game had been practised, we certainly are in it. We have simply been walked all over.[57]

Alms withdrew her financing for the sculpture, and on December 10, 1910, it was announced that Mr. and Mrs. Charles Phelps Taft had signed a $100,000 commission with the sculptor George Grey Barnard. Barnard took up the project enthusiastically and spent two years looking for a model who would approximate his vision of Lincoln, of whom he said, "He must have stood as the Republic should stand, strong, simple, carrying its weight unconsciously without pride in rank or culture. He is clothed with cloth worn, the history of labor."[58]

William Howard Taft had a particular interest in the memorial in Cincinnati, for he had earlier been appointed chairman of the Lincoln Memorial Commission to reanimate an association that had done little since it was created in 1867. After leaving the presidency in 1913, Taft became a professor of law at Yale and settled in New Haven, Connecticut, but retained his chairmanship of the Lincoln Commission. For ten more years Taft would play the role of mediator between various artistic and political factions. The Lincoln Memorial in Washington, a collaboration between the architect Henry Bacon, the muralist Jules Guérin, and the sculptor Daniel Chester French, was dedicated in 1922. Given Professor Taft's involvement in these matters, as well as the great reverence he inspired in Cincinnatians, he would be the only choice to deliver the dedicatory address for the unveiling of Barnard's *Lincoln* in Lytle Park on March 31, 1917.[59]

By 1916, when Barnard had completed his sculpture of Lincoln, the number of such monuments across the nation had grown to the point that a lively critical debate was held about how best to portray the great Republican hero. That this debate would also be played out against a background of international political revolutions and the imminent entrance of the United States into the war in Europe added a demagogic undertone to the aesthetic debate.

George Grey Barnard's notoriety as an artist with a near-mystical interpretation of the sculptor's role had earned him his share of detractors despite the patronage accorded him by the Rockefellers in 1915 for his work on the installation of the medieval stoneworks that would become the Cloisters in Fort Tryon Park, New York. Given his reputation, Barnard wanted to premier his *Lincoln* in New York City before shipping it to Ohio. On December 11, 1916, it was put on view at the Union Theological Seminary, and the debate was inaugurated by another former president, Theodore Roosevelt, who is recorded to have said, "I have always wished that I might see him; now I do."[60]

For a year the controversy continued, sparked mainly by rivalries among prominent sculptors and their apologists. Barnard's concept of a youthful Lincoln, unbearded and unmarked by either the cares or the presumed dignity of the presidency, was decried by the opposition, who claimed the statue was unsuitable for export as a symbolic representation of our nation. By midsummer of 1917, months after the March dedication in Cincinnati, it was learned that a cast of Barnard's *Lincoln* had been selected as a monument for London's Trafalgar Square to replace the previous selection of a Lincoln statue by Augustus Saint-Gaudens.[61]

During the years in which William Howard Taft had been giving his leadership to the Lincoln Memorial Commission in Washington, there were also projects underway to erect Lincoln statues in the capitals of France and Russia as well as Great Britain.[62] An Anglo-American committee had been formed in Great Britain to celebrate a century of peace between the two countries, but the preparations were suspended in 1914 because of the outbreak of war in Europe. Now, in 1917, thinking that he was dealing with the leadership of the American committee when he was approached, Charles Phelps Taft had agreed to underwrite the cost of a cast of the Barnard *Lincoln* for the Trafalgar Square monument. Saint-Gaudens's supporters were incensed by what they viewed as the treachery of the former president's wealthy brother, who would rob the sculptor of his rightfully won commission.[63] Ultimately, Taft's offer was rejected, and his gift was received instead by the people of Manchester, England, in 1919. A third cast, possibly intended by Barnard for Paris, never left the United States and ended up in Louisville, Kentucky.[64]

The years of the Barnard controversy, 1917 through 1919, coincide with the time in which the Tafts must have begun to think of the ultimate disposition of their collection. The planned gallery building across the street from their Pike Street residence never materialized, but included in the museum's documentary collection are drawings dated 1917 for an addition to the house that would have served as an annex for the display and storage of their holdings.[65] Apparently these plans, too, were abandoned. The fraternal correspondents, Charles Phelps and William Howard Taft, are disappointingly silent on the subject of the collection and its future. Their preserved letters from the last decade of their lives deal almost exclusively with family and financial matters, so one must presume that the family's discussions of art were held during their yearly reunions.

Evidence that Anna Sinton and Charles Phelps Taft took great pride in their achievements as collectors is the 1920 publication of a catalogue of the paintings collection privately commissioned from the writer Maurice Brockwell.[66] In addition to describing their holdings, Brockwell leads the reader on a room-by-room tour, showing his fine appreciation of the atmosphere the Tafts endeavored to create. Pointing out that the catalogue has been written for the use of visitors to the house, Brockwell also identifies the prominent characteristics of the collection in his introduction, which he subdivides into "The Portraits and Figure Pieces" and "The Landscapes." In a loquacious but informative style, Brockwell alludes tactfully to holes in the collection that the Tafts would later fill, such as a Gainsborough landscape, while offering anecdotal glimpses of the collectors' habits, which he must have gleaned from spending time with them.

In speaking of the portrait of Charles Frederick Fowles by Harrington Mann (see 1931.473, p. 222), Brockwell reminds the reader of the sitter's role in the formation of the Taft collection. Fowles and his wife had perished in the sinking of the steamship *Lusitania* in May 1915, and Taft had commissioned the posthumous painting to honor their association. Brockwell saluted the "clearness of Mr. Fowles's vision in realizing the aim of Mr. and Mrs. Taft . . . [which] is apparent to the merest tyro who may pay a visit to the house in Pike Street."[67]

Perhaps it was the loss of the friendly guidance of Fowles as well as the wartime atmosphere of the end of the decade that led the Tafts nearly to abandon collecting between 1916 and 1922. Only the 1918 purchase of Duveneck's *Cobbler's Apprentice* (see 1931.415, p. 292) stands out as a significant acquisition, and it might well be called a local event. But when they did return to the field, the Tafts made a number of purchases in all three major areas of the collection that confirmed the patterns that were already established.

With a sequence of purchases between 1920 and 1928, the Tafts made the most notable improvement in the field of Chinese porcelains. After a five-year hiatus, they began to enlarge their already sizable holdings of Kangxi porcelains with acquisitions from Parish-Watson and Company, New York. During six buying trips in a five-year period they purchased forty-six ceramics that remain in the collection, many of which bear illustrious provenances, including past ownership by James A. Garland, J. Pierpont Morgan, Richard Bennett, James W. Ellsworth, Mrs. Potter Palmer, and Henry Sampson. In his introduction to the entries on the porcelain collection, Anthony du Boulay describes the contemporary American passion for porcelains in which the Tafts participated.

The Tafts' advisers at the Parish-Watson gallery provided numerous famille verte and monochrome porcelains to supplement the existing strengths of the collection as well as six objects that provide antecedent examples for the Kangxi focus. Although Duveen had sold them twelve ceramics between 1902 and 1904 that were identified as Song (960–1279), Yuan (1271–1368), or Ming (1368–1644), only one of these acquisitions — the rare Wanli phoenix ewer with silver German mounts (see 1931.18, p. 575) — was retained. The Tafts later bought two Tang maidens (see 1931.143 and 1931.145, p. 574), dating between A.D. 618 and 907; a Liao vase from the eleventh or twelfth century (see 1931.144, pp. 574–75); and three large Ming vases of the *fahua*, or raised colors, type (see 1931.21–1931.23, pp. 576–77) from the Richard Bennett collection.

During this time the Tafts also acquired additional examples of highly prized shapes and glazes, presumably seeking out ceramics that could be paired with purchases previously made from Duveen or Clarke. These include another blue-and-white oviform jar with cover, also known as a ginger jar, decorated with prunus branches (see 1931.11, p. 578),[68] and an additional *langyao*, or oxblood, bottle vase (see 1931.105, p. 602). Perhaps the most significant purchase made from Parish-Watson was the garniture of famille noire baluster vases with covers and trumpet beakers from about 1710–20 (see 1931.148–152, pp. 670–71). The invoice, dated March 1, 1926, describes the grouping, formerly in the collections of J. Pierpont Morgan and his sister, Mrs. Walter Hayes Burns, and states that "this is the only complete garniture of its kind to exist in either private or public collections." More recently, a similar garniture, formerly in the collection of the princes of Liechtenstein, was donated to the Dallas Museum of Art.

From his early involvement in the formation of the Cincinnati Art Museum Association, Taft went on to serve as the president of the association from 1914 to 1927, during the tenure of Director Joseph Henry Gest (1859–1935). Gest was appointed director in 1902, and among his many duties numbered the directorship of the Rookwood Pottery. Established in 1880 by Maria Longworth Nichols Storer (1849–1932), daughter of Nicholas Longworth, and Joseph Bailey, Jr., on Longworth family properties atop Mount Adams, the pottery became world famous during the last two decades of the nineteenth century. By 1900 the popularity of Rookwood, with its hand-painted decorations derived from Storer's *japonisme*, began to wane as art potteries producing in the arts and crafts style became commercially established.

Although primary evidence is lacking to substantiate direct contacts between Rookwood artists and the Tafts, it is unimaginable that the artists were not frequently received on Pike Street where the growing collection of Asian objects would have drawn their attention. Taft's 1878 lecture on the purposes of art collecting for the inspiration of artists in one's own time and his relationship with Gest at the Cincinnati Art Museum would have facilitated such contact. In 1915 the Rookwood Pottery introduced the Soft Porcelain line, a new semitranslucent ceramic produced in simple shapes and covered with rich, single-color glazes to commemorate the thirty-fifth anniversary of the organization. The pottery's promotional literature for this new commercial line extolled the influence of ancient Chinese forms and glazes in an attempt to suggest modernity.[69]

In addition to Gest, the officers of the pottery at the time were John D. Wareham, head of the decorating department, and Stanley G. Burt, secretary of the company. In the *Catalog of Rookwood Art Pottery Shapes, 1907–1969*, Wareham and Burt are credited with the production of a number of designs that recall the shapes of Chinese porcelains in the Taft collection.[70] In one instance Wareham is documented as the originator of a vase (shape 2267) whose shape closely resembles the Taft Museum's imperial Qianlong beaker vase (see 1931.115, pp. 607–8).

Founding of the Taft Museum

Having expended such large amounts of cash and concern on the creation of their collections, Charles Phelps and Anna Sinton Taft might be expected to have given no less consideration to establishing the museum that now bears their name. Their earlier plans to erect structures separate from their residence in which to house the collection no doubt proceeded from their knowledge of museum practices and the need to ensure proper display and maintenance of the works of art. It is likely that Taft and Gest discussed the ultimate dispensation of the family collection and that they had mutually agreed that the residence on Pike Street would remain its repository.

To establish the museum the Tafts decided to create a single foundation that would embrace their cultural interests in both music and the visual arts, to be called the Cincinnati Institute of Fine Arts. They would give to this foundation one million dollars as well as the house and their collection, provided that the citizens of Cincinnati would raise two and a half million dollars, thereby creating an endowment to sustain the museum and to provide operating support to the Cincinnati Symphony Orchestra, the Conservatory of Music, and the Cincinnati Art Museum. Documents were drawn up and signed in 1927, and, with the required matching funds in hand, the institute was established. By this plan the Tafts would live in the house until their deaths, at which time it would cease to be a private residence and become a public museum.

After Charles Phelps Taft died on December 31, 1929, Mrs. Taft faced the task of fulfilling the couple's pledge. Gest's retirement the following year left vacant both the directorship of the Cincinnati Art Museum and the stewardship of the future Taft Museum. Fortunately for both institutions this vacancy was soon filled by a well-qualified individual, Walter P. Siple (1890–1978), who assumed both challenges with enthusiasm. After his appointment, Siple must have met with Mrs. Taft, who would have shared with him her late husband's great pride in the accumulation of their treasures. It is regrettable that no precise information on their discussions or the origins of his plans for the museum's renovation remains. When Siple resigned from the Cincinnati Art Museum in 1949 he took with him all his personal papers and correspondence, and efforts to recover this archive at the time of his death were unsuccessful.

The loss of documents that might have substantiated the nature of Siple's vision of the future Taft Museum is partially compensated by correspondence and notes in the Taft Museum's files, which Siple did not remove. From these papers it is possible to see how Siple organized the renovation so that the house would reflect an elegant federal-period residence. Through the choice of wall colors, carpets, draperies, and American furniture integrated with the architecture of the 1820 building, Siple and the architect Woodward Garber established an environment for the European treasures that the Tafts had collected. Thus, all the Tafts' own furniture, excepting two eighteenth-century French commodes (see 1931.333 and 1931.334, pp. 554 and 555), was removed, and the Victorian-era moldings and fireplaces were replaced with historical reproductions and authentic period mantelpieces salvaged from decaying houses in the vicinity. This process of renovation is described in greater detail both by Cote and by Lisa Krieger in her essay "Furniture and Interior Decoration at the Taft Museum."

In addition to the renovation, Siple made another significant contribution to the new museum: the publication of a handbook to guide viewers through the rooms where the collection was displayed. There are indications that Siple saw this volume, issued in 1939, as a preliminary publication that would be followed by a more comprehensive catalogue.

By the time of Siple's resignation, the daily operations of the Taft Museum were in the charge of a curator, Katherine Hanna, whose appointment signaled the increasing autonomy of the two museums. When she was made director of the Taft Museum in 1951, the independence of the two institutions was confirmed. By the late 1950s, when Siple's handbook was out of print, Hanna organized its republication, adding bibliographic citations and loan histories where appropriate.

In their deed of gift Mr. and Mrs. Taft had made their feelings on the maintenance of the integrity of their collection clear. Works of art could be added but would have to be shown separately from their donations. They stated explicitly that they did not wish their collection to rival that of the Cincinnati Art Museum: rather, it should be an adjunct to that institution. However, when the Tafts' two daughters died in 1962, leaving gifts of art, including the painting *At the Piano* by J. A. M. Whistler (see 1962.7, p. 218), to the Taft Museum, the trustees of the Cincinnati Institute of Fine Arts recognized the need to make exceptions to this policy so as to accept and integrate them with the Tafts' own objects.[71] The death in 1972 of Hulbert Taft, a favorite nephew, brought the museum an impressive dining table of New York manufacture from about 1810–20 (see 1977.1, p. 100).

A further obstacle to the acceptance of additional gifts has been the adherence to Siple's original installation of the collection, which had utilized all available display space and been tied to the room-by-room format of the 1939 and 1958 handbooks. The present publication reflects the recent decision to rearrange portions of the collection and to set aside an area where any future gifts might be displayed. In 1987 the trustees approved an acquisitions policy for the museum that permits the addition of objects that merit inclusion on the basis of demonstrated relevance to the core collection and that uphold its standards of quality. Thus, in 1988, the museum was able to accept an oil sketch for Farny's *Song of the Talking Wire* (see 1988.1, p. 300).

The Sinton fortune that Annie had inherited and that Charles had helped her to administer had been based on large real-estate holdings in Cincinnati as well as in Texas and in other parts of the country. The Tafts, therefore, were familiar with the vagaries of land development and even witnessed in their own lifetimes the alteration of the Pike Street neighborhood from the exclusive residential district it had been at the turn of the century to a manufacturing and mixed-use area by the mid-1920s.[72] Cognizant that after their deaths they could in no way ensure the future of the 1820 residence, their deed of gift explicitly allowed the art collection to be moved to another building if the trustees of the Cincinnati Institute of Fine Arts deemed such action necessary to safeguard the collection.[73]

During Hanna's administration, which continued until 1983, the Taft Museum did sustain several challenges to its future well-being. It was occasionally rumored that for reasons of community economy the Cincinnati Art Museum would absorb the Taft collection, a rumor that gained substance with the visible deterioration of the Lytle Park neighborhood where the museum is located. By the early 1960s the Taft Museum was more seriously threatened by the planned construction of an interstate freeway that was to go through Lytle Park at grade level, isolating the museum from the edge of the downtown area it had long graced.[74] Fortunately, civic leaders rallied to save the district and with it the museum's location by compelling federal officials to accept a plan to create a tunnel beneath Lytle Park.

From that time forward the Lytle Park area has been revitalized, and the museum is well integrated in the fabric of the district, which is now influenced by the international headquarters of the Procter & Gamble Company and other corporations. To the east, behind the museum, a new residential and office complex is being developed, and Sawyer Park, a riverfront recreational area, was created as part of the city's bicentennial celebrations in 1988. These private and public investments offer the Taft Museum a sense of serenity as it enters its seventh decade.

Great American Family Collections and the Taft Museum

Although their collection was clearly more modest, one may yet wish to compare the Tafts with the collectors Isabella Stewart Gardner (1840–1924) in Boston and Henry Clay Frick (1849–1919) in Pittsburgh and New York. All were actively collecting at the same time and were pursued by some of the same vendors, who tried to spark rivalries among their American clients. Even the journalists of the day were involved in stimulating the appearance of competition, as Gardner noted in a letter to her adviser, Bernard Berenson, written August 11, 1909: "We are rather amused by a newspaper account of the Great Collections in America. It eliminates Morgan's because so much of it is in Europe and goes on to say the 3 great ones are Frick's, Widener's and Charles Taft's. No hope for me."[75]

Superficially, Gardner appears to have been a more adventuresome collector than the others, although Frick had the greatest wealth. Gardner and Frick were also emboldened by the more numerous examples of earlier Bostonians and New Yorkers who had enriched their respective cities with great private collections. By contrast, as a founder and then president of the Cincinnati Art Museum Association, Taft, along with his wife, was acutely aware of just how thinly spread the visual-arts resources of Cincinnati were during the first quarter of this century. The Tafts began to collect only after David Sinton's death, when they were already into middle age, and they assembled the collection to provide appropriate examples of schools, styles, and techniques where virtually none existed. And, so long as they chose to remain on Pike Street, the space limitations of the house would pose major restrictions.

Isabella Stewart Gardner offered the Tafts a superb model on which to base their projections toward the creation of a museum housing a private collection. That they took note of her activities is substantiated by a file in the museum's archives that contains newspaper reports of the opening of her museum in Boston in January 1903. Gardner's wealth, possessions, and ambitions were such that only a specifically constructed building would suffice to display her collection according to her vision and aesthetic principles.[76] She had enormous advantages as the adored wife of John L. (Jack) Gardner, living in Boston with its rich educational resources, and beginning to collect during the decade of the 1880s under the tutelage of such men as Henry James, James Abbott McNeill Whistler, John Singer Sargent, and artists living in Boston. She bought her first old-master painting in 1888,[77] and when she inherited a legacy of nearly two million dollars from her father in 1891, she was ready to establish a collection that would equal those of the Italian palazzos she loved to visit.

Henry Clay Frick had none of the early educational or cultural advantages that were shared by Isabella Stewart Gardner and Charles and Annie Taft. His youthful experiences were more like those of David Sinton, since Frick was the child of Pennsylvania farmers and had little formal education.[78] Working as a teenager in a business owned by relatives of his mother, he recognized the future of the coke-making business for the steel industry of Pittsburgh and in 1871 borrowed enough money to join his cousins in partnership to buy a coal tract and finance the building of coke ovens. Their business survived and prospered in that decade, so that by 1878 Frick, having earlier bought out his partners, reorganized the business as

H. C. Frick and Company.[79] By 1880 its owner was a millionaire at the age of thirty-one and ready to embark on his first trip to Europe accompanied by Andrew Mellon and two other Pittsburgh friends.

Visits to European museums and private art collections encouraged Frick to develop a taste for art, which he had already displayed in the 1870s, although his earliest purchases are unrecorded. After his marriage in 1881 Frick chose works of art to decorate the couple's first apartment, and when they bought an Italianate house in 1882, the pace of his purchasing accelerated. Over the years, extensive remodeling of the house, called Clayton, offered opportunities to reinstall and enlarge his collection of paintings, furniture, and decorative arts. The reorganization of his business interests in 1900, through a buy out of his holdings, left Frick immensely wealthy and prompted him to relocate to residences in Massachusetts and New York City, where he rented the Vanderbilt mansion on Fifth Avenue in 1905. According to his daughter, Helen Clay Frick, he was deeply impressed by the Wallace Collection in London, which he had seen on his first European tour, and, following that model, planned to build a residence destined to be a public museum to show his collection. The house was ready for occupancy by 1914, and in the years before his death five years later, Frick increased its magnificence with a number of outstanding purchases. The Frick Collection opened to the public in 1935, three years after the opening of the Taft Museum.

Ultimately, it is the perfect amalgam of collection and location that makes the Taft Museum unique and distinguishes it from the quixotic grandeur of the Gardner and the baronial majesty of the Frick. In the conservative and self-effacing environment of this Ohio River town, the Taft's display strikes a chord of harmony as it accommodates the preservation of a historic structure and the conservation of a collection formed mainly for provincial edification. It is worth recalling that in the document establishing the Cincinnati Institute of Fine Arts and its dependency, the Taft Museum, the founders stated that the Cincinnati Art Museum should be the principal museum of their city and that their own benefaction should be but an adjunct. Such serene confidence in the intrinsic value of their possessions is perhaps the best testimony of what eye, heart, and spirit can accomplish even on the furthermost frontier of the eastern United States.

Notes

1. *Cincinnati Enquirer*, Dec. 5, 1873.

2. "David Sinton," *Cincinnati, the Queen City: Pictorial and Biographical*, vol. 1, Cincinnati, 1912, pp. 13–16. See also David Sinton Papers, Cincinnati Historical Society.

3. See James D. McCabe, Jr., *Great Fortunes and How They Were Made*, Cincinnati, 1871, and Abby S. Schwartz, "Nicholas Longworth: Art Patron of Cincinnati," *The Taft Museum: A Cincinnati Legacy*, Cincinnati, 1988. See also Nicholas Longworth Papers and Hiram Powers Papers, Cincinnati Historical Society.

4. Benjamin West (1738–1820), *Ophelia and Laertes*, 1792, oil on canvas, 109 x 152 in., is now in the collection of the Cincinnati Art Museum, gift of Joseph Longworth, inv. no. 1882.230.

5. Ishbel Ross, *An American Family*, Cleveland, 1964, is the indispensable guide to the William Howard Taft collection of papers in the Library of Congress. Using the family's correspondence, Ross recounts the Tafts' history from 1678 to 1964.

6. Mrs. Willa Beall, former executive director of the William Howard Taft Memorial Association in Cincinnati, corresponded with Ishbel Ross and supplied details of family life not found in the presidential papers. Ross's account of Annie's childhood is based on the recollections of a Sinton-Taft domestic worker who was alive in the 1960s. During her later life Annie Sinton Taft did not wish to divulge her age, and her birth date cannot be confirmed. I have used the archives of Spring Grove Cemetery, which record her birth in 1852.

7. Annie's name is not recorded in a list of students published in the school's journal, *The Mount Auburn Index* (1870–72).

8. David Sinton Taft died of typhoid fever in 1891. Charles Howard Taft suffered a nervous breakdown after his college years and afterward lived in Providence, Rhode Island, where he died in 1931.

9. Ross, chaps. 8 and 9, summarizes this period.

10. See the obituary of Charles Phelps Taft published by the *Cincinnati Times-Star*, Dec. 30, 1929. See also the centennial issue of the *Times-Star* and clippings in the archives of the *Cincinnati Post*.

11. William Howard Taft Papers, series 1, Library of Congress, Washington, D.C. (hereinafter referred to as WHT Papers). See especially Peter Rawson Taft's letters to Alphonso Taft written from Heidelberg, Berlin, and Paris between May 16, 1868, and May 31, 1870.

12. WHT Papers, Oct. 8, 1900.

13. Charles P. Taft, *The South Kensington Museum: What It Is; How It Originated; What It Has Done and Is Now Doing for England and the World; and the Adaptation of Such an Institution to the Needs and Possibilities of This City*, Cincinnati, 1878, pp. 6–7.

14. Taft, p. 36.

15. Taft, p. 37.

16. Taft, p. 40.

17. Taft, pp. 41–42.

18. Cincinnati Art Museum, *The Ladies, God Bless 'Em: The Women's Art Movements in Cincinnati in the Nineteenth Century*, Cincinnati, 1976, and Millard F. Rogers, Jr., et al., *Art Palace of the West: A Centennial Tribute, 1881–1981*, Cincinnati, 1981.

19. Millard F. Rogers, Jr., "Mary M. Emery: Development of an American Collector," *Bulletin of the Cincinnati Art Museum*, vol. XIII, no. 3 (Dec. 1986), pp. 4–19.

20. Letter from Charles Taft to William Howard Taft, June 10, 1901, WHT Papers. All letters cited in this essay are from Charles to William, unless otherwise noted.

21. WHT Papers, Nov. 6, 1902. The paintings mentioned in the letter can be identified, on the basis of the 1902 catalogue (see note 22), as follows: Meissonier's *Three Friends* (see 1931.399, p. 236) and Corot's *Brook beneath the Trees with a House in the Distance* (see 1931.438, p. 251) and *Peasants Stopping at the Edge of a Wooded Road near a Village* (formerly *At Ville-d'Avray*) (see 1931.437, p. 249), which remain in the collection; and Gainsborough's *Grand Landscape*, Constable's *On the Stour*, Troyon's *Le Bac*, Diaz's *Forest of Fontainebleau*, and Vibert's *A Morning Gossip*, now no longer in the collection.

22. C. F. Fowles, *The Art Collection of Mr. and Mrs. Charles P. Taft, Cincinnati, Ohio*, New York, 1902.

23. See note 21 for the works by Gainsborough, Constable, and Troyon; in addition, Dupré's *Silvery Moonlight* and Ziem's *Grand Canal, Venice* were replaced by other works by the same artists.

24. The seven paintings that remain in the collection from the 1902 catalogue are those listed in note 21 as well as Vibert's *Cardinal* (see 1931.469, p. 246), Daubigny's *Evening Solitude* (see 1931.426, p. 270) and *Evening on the Oise* (see 1931.462, p. 00), and Fortuny's *Arab Guard* (see 1931.430, p. 229).

25. John Getz, *A Catalogue of Chinese Porcelains Collected by Mr. and Mrs. Charles P. Taft*, New York, 1904.

26. The tapestries are *Adoration of the Magi* (see 1931.332, p. 547), *The Flute Player*, and *The Dream of Rinaldo*, the latter two after François Boucher (see 1931.330 and 1931.331, pp. 550 and 551); the Limoges ewers are by Jean de Court (see 1931.290 and 1931.292, pp. 384 and 385–86).

27. The current attributions of the Tafts' "della Robbias" are as follows: workshop of Benedetto Buglioni, *Virgin and Child*, ca. 1490 (see 1931.316, p. 465); followers of the della Robbia, *The Virgin and Saint Joseph Adoring the Christ Child*, sixteenth and nineteenth or twentieth century (see 1931.321, p. 467); and imitator of the della Robbia, *Bust of a Child*, nineteenth century (see 1931.315, p. 467).

28. Letter from Charles Fowles to Charles Taft, Nov. 19, 190[2], in Taft Museum files. Although this letter bears a date that might also be read "1903," information in the body of the letter confirms a date of 1902.

29. June 24, 1910, WHT Papers.

30. Dec. 8, 1902, WHT Papers.

31. Dec. 26, 1902, WHT Papers.

32. Letter from William Howard Taft to Charles Taft, Jan. 26, 1903, WHT Papers.

33. Feb. 11, 1903, WHT Papers.

34. See note 28. This is the first letter from Fowles on the Scott and Fowles letterhead.

35. Apr. 18, 1903, WHT Papers. The invoice for these paintings is missing; however, the paintings mentioned can be tentatively identified as Jacob Maris's *Rotterdam* (see 1931.458, p. 281), Rousseau's *Pond (La Mare)* (formerly *Evening: Fontainebleau*; see 1931.429, p. 260), and Reynolds's *Miss Ridge*. Invoices in the Taft Museum archives show that the Lhermitte was sold in 1905 through Scott and Fowles, but its subject cannot be identified.

36. S. N. Behrman, *Duveen*, New York, 1951, rev. ed, 1982; Colin Simpson, *Artful Partners*, New York, 1986.

37. Vendors' statements in the archives of the Taft Museum.

38. Correspondence in the archives of the Taft Museum.

39. The Rosselino is identified as a Madonna and Child in the archives of the Taft Museum.

40. The Botticelli was a portrait from the collection of Frizzoni of Borgamino. Letter from Willem von Bode to Charles Taft, July 27, 1907, in Taft Museum files.

41. July 12, 1903, WHT Papers. The painting by Constant Troyon is *Cattle at a Watering Place* (see 1931.465, p. 256).

42. July 31, 1903, WHT Papers. These purchases cannot be specifically identified because there are no corresponding invoices in the Taft Museum archives.

43. Oct. 19, 1903, WHT Papers.

44. Although the Ziem cannot be identified, the Gainsborough is *Portrait of an Unknown Man* (now ascribed to a late-eighteenth- or early-nineteenth-century imitator; see 1931.397, p. 183).

45. Mar. 19, 1904, WHT Papers.

46. Oct. 20, 1904, WHT Papers.

47. May 4, 1905, WHT Papers.

48. Correspondence in the archives of the Taft Museum.

49. The portrait attributed to Anthony van Dyck at the time of purchase is now ascribed to an imitator of Van Dyck, ca. 1900.

50. According to the 1902 catalogue, the Tafts formerly owned *The Confirmation* by Dagnan-Bouveret, *Checkmated* by Charles Léon-Herrmann, and *A Morning Gossip* by Vibert; the only religious subjects presently in the collection are Isabey's *Communicants* (1931.417, p. 244), purchased in 1905, and Vibert's *Cardinal* (1931.469, p. 246), purchased in 1902.

51. Ross, chap. 15.

52. May 13, 1909, WHT Papers.

53. *The Cincinnati Magazine*, Sept. 1909, p. 22.

54. Clippings in the archives of the Taft Museum.

55. *Cincinnati Museum Association's Thirty-First Annual Report for the Year Ending December 31, 1911*, Cincinnati, 1912, pp. 20–21.

56. Constable's *Dedham Mill* is now known as *Landscape with Canal*, ca. 1820–60, by Frederick Waters Watts.

57. Dec. 9, 1910, WHT Papers.

58. George Grey Barnard, "The Sculptor's View of Lincoln," in *Barnard's Lincoln*, Cincinnati, 1917, p. 26.

59. *Barnard's Lincoln*, p. 33, contains the full text of his address.

60. "George Grey Barnard's Statue of Lincoln," *Outlook*, vol. cxiv, no. 27 (Dec. 1916), p. 891.

61. F. L. Bullard, *Lincolns in Marble and Bronze*, New Jersey, 1952, pp. 228–41.

62. Frederick C. Moffatt, "Pirated Patronage: The Tafts and George Grey Barnard's *Lincoln*," in *Abstracts and Program Statements*, College Art Association, 1990 Annual Conference, New York, pp. 136–37.

63. "Quarreling over Lincoln's Statue," *Literary Digest* (Oct. 13, 1917), p. 30.

64. Bullard, p. 240.

65. 1917 drawing in the archives of the Taft Museum.

66. Maurice W. Brockwell, *A Catalogue of Paintings in the Collection of Mr. and Mrs. Charles P. Taft at Cincinnati, Ohio*, New York, 1920.

67. Brockwell, p. 200.

68. For a discussion of the purchase of the two ginger jars, see Anthony Derham, "Blue-and-White at a Price," *Apollo*, n.s., vol. cxxviii, no. 322 (Dec. 1988), pp. 406–7.

69. From his research on Rookwood pottery, Kenneth R. Trapp of the Oakland Museum was able to point out, in a telephone conversation, the Chinese influence on Rookwood pottery manifested in the line of soft-paste porcelain. See also Garth Clark, *American Ceramics: 1876 to the Present*, New York, 1988, p. 286.

70. *Catalog of Rookwood Art Pottery Shapes, 1907–1969*, Kingston, N.Y., 1973, vol. ii.

71. The 1962 bequests from the Tafts' daughters are inventory numbers 1962.1–11.

72. See scrapbooks and manuscripts by Charles J. Livingood (1866–1952) and Anna Fostor Haines in the Cincinnati Historical Society for background information on the demolition of the Lytle residence ca. 1904–10 to create a park for downtown workers. See also correspondence in WHT Papers cited above about the building of the Pugh Building next to the Baum-Taft House.

73. Deed of Gift, article 3.D.

74. Jana C. Morford, "Preserving a 'Special Place': The Lytle Park Neighborhood, 1848–1976," *Queen City Heritage*, vol. xliv, no. 3 (Fall 1986), pp. 3–22.

75. *The Letters of Bernard Berenson and Isabella Stewart Gardner*, ed. Rollin Van N. Hadley, Boston, 1987, p. 452.

76. Rollin Van N. Hadley, *Museums Discovered: The Isabella Stewart Gardner Museum*, Florida, 1981, introduction, n.p.

77. Hadley identifies this painting as a *Madonna and Child*, formerly attributed to Zurbarán.

78. Information in these paragraphs is drawn from *Clayton*, exh. cat., Helen Clay Frick Foundation, Pittsburgh, 1988, containing essays by Joanne B. Moore, Ellen M. Rosenthal, and Kahren Jones Hellerstadt.

79. Hellerstadt, in *Clayton*, p. 62, quotes the famous assessment of young Frick made by a Pittsburgh banker, "Lands good, ovens well built; manager on job all day, keeps books evenings, may be a little too enthusiastic about pictures but not enough to hurt; knows his business down to the ground; advise making the loan."

The Baum-Taft House:
An Architectural History

Richard C. Cote

The Baum-Taft House is one of the oldest surviving wooden structures in Cincinnati. Significant in southwestern Ohio for its age and style, the building, known today as the Taft Museum, was built by 1820 for the Cincinnati merchant Martin Baum. Its subsequent owners, especially Nicholas Longworth, David Sinton, and Mr. and Mrs. Charles Phelps Taft, transformed the house into a stellar example of nineteenth-century architectural eclecticism, before its 1930s restoration as the Taft Museum. As is true of any artifact of material culture, the Baum-Taft House must be studied within the context of the eras in which it was both built and altered. Historians, therefore, must first turn to Martin Baum and the village of Cincinnati to understand the structure that subsequent owners enlarged and renovated.

Martin Baum came to Cincinnati sometime in the early 1790s; his name appears in the records of the First Presbyterian Church of Cincinnati for July 11, 1794.[1] Another church record, the birth and baptismal registry of the Salem Reformed Church (now the United Church of Christ) of Hagerstown, Maryland, lists his birth on June 15, 1765.[2] The *Cincinnati City Directory* of 1825, however, contradicts this information and lists his birthplace as "Pennsylvania." Regardless of where Baum was born, in Maryland or Pennsylvania, he came to southwestern Ohio from an area that had been settled well before Cincinnati was, one with a well-established tradition of domestic architecture, which would—consciously or unconsciously—influence his future building activity.

During the first decade of Baum's residence in Cincinnati, the village had a population of five hundred residents living in ninety-four cabins and ten frame houses. To this Baum added his own two-story frame dwelling and a general store, the business by which he soon became one of the area's wealthiest citizens. In 1803 he expanded his business by helping to form the Miami Exporting Company, which later became the first bank in Ohio. Baum eventually served as its first president. Confident in his economic success, in 1804 Baum married Ann Sommerville Wallace, a union that brought him social prominence. As a measure of his economic and social status, Baum erected a new brick residence adjacent to his store at Front and Sycamore streets. Here, the couple lived until they built the Baum-Taft House fifteen years later.

Baum's business interests expanded to include a sugar refinery, iron foundry, and steam mill. In 1817 he was elected a director of the Cincinnati branch of the Bank of the United States. With his economic status seemingly assured, Baum directed his energies to community improvements. His name appears in connection with the Lancastrian Society, the Cincinnati College, the Cincinnati Literary Society, the Western Museum, and the Apollonian Society. He was an active member of the Society for the Promotion of Agriculture, Manufacturing, and the Domestic Economy and served as a trustee of the Select Council of the city corporation.

Baum was also involved in Cincinnati land speculation and owned numerous parcels throughout the growing town. On September 1, 1812, he purchased from Daniel Symmes a lot of nine acres "this side of Deer Creek."[3] Here, on a tract that would eventually become part of downtown Cincinnati, Baum planted a garden around 1817–18, two years before he erected a new dwelling.[4]

The new residence is first mentioned in a letter Baum wrote to William Lytle on August 22, 1820, in which he offered to sell "my Deercreek land, including the new House and all the materials thereon for $30,600."[5] The "new House" is the Baum-Taft House, which had been erected on the nine-acre parcel that Baum had purchased in 1812. Baum's sale of his new dwelling so soon after building it was due to the national financial depression of 1820. A panic in Cincinnati occurred when the Bank of the United States in Washington failed to recognize notes of collateral sent to it by its Cincinnati branch. The notes were issued primarily against land, and Baum, with his vast speculative holdings, was especially hard hit and was thus forced to sell his new residence.

The house that Martin Baum built in 1820 was the product of a Cincinnati much changed from the one he first knew in the 1790s. In 1819 Cincinnati had a population of just over 10,000 citizens, who lived and worked in 1,890 buildings, 1,003 of which were designated as residences. Of these, 843 buildings were one-story and 615 were two-story structures of wood.[6] Thus, Martin Baum's "new House" of wood conformed to the majority of small wood-frame structures in Cincinnati in 1819. Unfortunately, the growth and prosperity of Cincinnati have virtually eliminated the city's other contemporary dwellings, and early descriptions and photographs are all that remain of the city's early-nineteenth-century buildings.

The historical and architectural contexts of the Baum-Taft House are further revealed in an early printed source, *Leading Manufacturers and Merchants of Cincinnati and Environs*. Published in 1886, *Leading Manufacturers and Merchants* was written as a reminiscence and serves as an astoundingly precise source of information on the city's early architecture. Under the heading "Historical Places and Landmarks" the author noted, "The pioneers built log-houses for defense and shelter, but they were only of a temporary character." It was not until the earliest settlers prospered that the residences began to reflect higher architectural aspirations within their communities. The author noted a change in Cincinnati's buildings when he wrote: "A few small windowed two-storied houses yet remain of those built in the second period of houses in this city." The Baum-Taft House belongs to this "second period," to which the author provided the following information:

> The elements of the population that held Virginia traditions built, between 1825–30, several fine houses in the semi-classical style, the oldest being the Key's House, where Charles McMicken lived, and a part of which may yet be seen in front of the University of Cincinnati building. . . . In much the same style is the house now owned and occupied by David Sinton, on the east side of Pike Street, almost opposite the east end of Fourth. The house was begun by Martin Baum and finished by Nicholas Longworth, who died there. It is a one-story house, very wide and deep, with a broad hall through the centre resting on a half-story or basement. The place has always been known as the gathering spot for the culture and refinement of the city.[7]

Although Martin Baum did not come from Virginia, the comparison the author made between the Baum residence and a "Virginia tradition" is both interesting and valid. The fact that the comment was made in 1886, when the Taft House was sixty-six years old, makes the reference to the architecture of Virginia all the more compelling. The story-and-a-half-size house, in many ways refined by Thomas Jefferson at Monticello, was a popular building form

Fig. 1 The Pike Street façade of the Baum-Taft House from *Memorial of the Golden Wedding of Nicholas Longworth and Susan Longworth Celebrated at Cincinnati on Christmas Eve, 1857.* Color lithograph by Hunckel & Son, Baltimore.

Fig. 2 Stono, Virginia three-part Palladian plan house, John Jordon and Samuel Darst, builders, 1818. Lexington, Va.

by the time that Baum erected his "new House." The earliest view of the Baum-Taft House, published in 1857, shows the façade and arched double doorway dominated by a pedimented Doric portico, the main block of five bays ornamented with elliptical attic windows (fig. 1). Extending from the main block are two single-story wings. The house conforms stylistically to its Virginia prototype, and the interior plan underscores the similarity (fig. 2). The author of *Leading Manufacturers* noted that the house was "very wide and deep, with a broad hall through the centre resting on a half-story or basement."[8] This is the conventional Virginia central-passage plan, with the large hall used for ventilation and circulation in the heat and humidity of a southern summer. If, as previously suggested, Martin Baum was indeed from Maryland, he could have seen the same plan in Homewood, the Charles Carroll mansion in Baltimore, the most prominent example of the type in his native state.

It is clear that the general design of Baum's "new House" combined several architectural sources: the Virginia-Maryland style and Cincinnati's vernacular building tradition. Yet to go beyond a regional context and to ask who specifically designed and built Baum's house is to explore nineteenth-century American building practices.

Determining who built the Baum House is particularly complex because it has been attributed to several prominent American architects. As early as 1887 the *Inland Architect and News Record* named Benjamin Henry Latrobe as the architect of the house.[9] The attribution was maintained by the prominent American architectural historian and critic Montgomery Schuyler, who in 1908 published in the *Architectural Record* the following statement:

> The house which Martin Baum built in Cincinnati in 1817, and for which he was well inspired to choose for his architect Benjamin H. Latrobe, then fulfilling the last year of his service as architect of the Capitol at Washington. It is quite unmistakably Latrobe's, to those who know the work that he was doing in Baltimore and elsewhere in those years, and who remember his insistence, in design as well as in words, upon "simplicity" as the first of architectural qualities.[10]

Other authorities, among them the distinguished art and architectural historian Fiske Kimball, further supported this attribution. In an article published in *Art and Archaeology* in 1919, Kimball discussed the Baum-Taft House in light of Schuyler's earlier comments:

> Always admired, the house attracted the attention of the late Montgomery Schuyler, a leader in the study of American architecture, who ascribed the authorship of its design to Benjamin Latrobe. The attribution is indeed a tempting one, especially as Latrobe was in Pittsburgh from 1811 to 1814, and is reported by his son to have furnished designs for several houses along the Ohio. Although no preserved examples of domestic buildings surely designed by him, which might serve as reliable terms of comparison, have been identified, there is a certain affinity in the window treatment and other features of the Cincinnati house with details in some of Latrobe's public buildings.[11]

While Kimball would later retract his attribution, other historians continued to suggest Latrobe's involvement in the design of the Baum-Taft House. In the classic and popular work *Early Homes of Ohio*, I. T. Frary wrote of the house: "Local tradition names as the architect James Hoban, who designed the White House at Washington, but better grounds exist for attributing it to Benjamin Henry Latrobe."[12]

Although recent studies have proven that the attributions to Hoban and Latrobe are unfounded, such ascriptions to prominent American architects are by no means unique to the Baum-Taft House. Scholarship in American architectural history has until recently focused on the best-known architects and builders. From these early studies many buildings possessing similar characteristics have been assigned to prominent figures, virtually ignoring lesser-known contemporary practitioners in smaller cities such as Cincinnati.

When the Baum-Taft House was built around 1820, Cincinnati already had its own building community, which could and in fact did provide the talent for both the design and the construction of Martin Baum's "new House." The *Cincinnati Directory* for 1819 provides valuable insight into the local building community, noting that there were "between 80 and 100 principal house carpenters and joiners, employing about 400 journey men and apprentices."

This is a significant number of house carpenters and a very large support system. The directory also recorded "twenty-five [brick] yards employing, during the season for making brick, about 200 workmen."[13] In addition, the directory listed 100 bricklayers, 30 plasterers, and 15 stonemasons. Thus, in a city with a population of just over 10,000 citizens, 800 men were engaged in the building trade. Curiously, however, the directory does not list a single architect for a city that had 1,890 buildings, of which 1,003 were dwellings.

Thus, it seems clear that the builder of Martin Baum's residence would have come from Cincinnati's own building community. It should be emphasized that most residences built in the United States during the early nineteenth century were not executed from the designs of architects. Rather, they were the products of local builders who were trained as either carpenters or masons. Such builders, working during this period, typically did not call themselves "architects." Moreover, their clients, men like Martin Baum, had little or no understanding of the architectural profession and simply saw builders—that is, carpenters and masons—as workmen, men who performed tasks that required a specific skill. The aspirations of the client, in this instance Martin Baum, determined the type and complexity of the structure.

Based on English precedent and tradition, the builder in early-nineteenth-century America had several available sources for the design of his buildings. The first, and by far the most popular, was the architectural handbook. When Baum erected his residence, American carpenters, most notably Asher Benjamin of Boston and Owen Biddle of Philadelphia, had published books for their fellow carpenters and masons to provide architectural information that could be incorporated into building projects, both public and private. Retailed in most American cities and universally accepted, Benjamin's and Biddle's works contained instruction on the orders of architecture, drawings of plans and elevations, and building components, as well as methods of building construction popular in the eastern United States.

It would have been extremely unusual and atypical of Cincinnati's building community not to have had the works of both Benjamin and Biddle at hand. Certain exterior details visible in the earliest (1857) view of the house make specific references to the classicism found in both pattern books. The portico dominating the façade, faithfully executed in the Roman Doric order, suggests the influence of an architectural handbook. Moreover, the elliptical windows of the attic story were popularized by both Benjamin and Biddle, pirated in turn from English sources of the same period.

Further, a significant portion of the early-nineteenth-century composition plasterwork found on the ceilings of the principal rooms of the Baum-Taft House has survived. This architectural component is an important statement not only of the architectural aspirations of Martin Baum but also of the capabilities and construction methods of Cincinnati's building community. Who was responsible for these important details? Again, the answer may be found in the 1819 *Cincinnati Directory*, which listed thirty plasterers. The plasterwork may have originated with this group, since plasterers were typically responsible for the installation of composition plaster ornaments. There are two possible explanations as to how the extant ceiling medallions found their way into the Baum-Taft House. They were either manufactured in the East and shipped to a builder in Cincinnati for installation or made by a local plasterer from designs found in a builder's guide. Both options merit consideration.

The most popular source for prefabricated plasterwork was the Philadelphia plaster manufacturer Robert Wellford. Indeed, at the time the Baum residence was constructed, Robert Wellford's manufacturing operation was at its peak. Wellford had begun advertising composition plaster in the *Philadelphia City Directory* in 1802 and continued to do so until 1836. In an undated advertisement in the Historical Society of Pennsylvania, Wellford explains the virtues of plaster ornament: "A cheap substitute for wood carving has long been desirable for some situations, particularly enriched mouldings, etc. and various were the attempts to answer the purpose, the last and most successful is usually termed composition ornament." Wellford went on to note that plaster "is a cement of solid and tenacious materials, which when properly incorporated and pressed into moulds receives a fine relief; in the drying it becomes hard as stone, strong and durable, so as to answer most effectually the general purpose of wood carving and not likely to chip." Wellford indicated that he would ship his plasterwork anywhere on the continent with "a generous allowance made to whole-sale purchasers, with printed directions for fixing the composition gratis."[14] Wellford's promotions were successful, and his composition plasterwork has survived in buildings throughout the East Coast. Attribution to him can be made on the basis of signed examples or from surviving written documentation, such as receipts. Unfortunately, since the Baum-Taft House plasterwork lacks both forms of evidence, a secure attribution to Wellford is impossible.

Alternatively, the Baum-Taft plasterwork may have been made locally and inspired by an architectural publication. The most likely candidate is Asher Benjamin and Daniel Raynerd's *American Builder's Companion*, first published in Boston in 1806 and widely circulated and reprinted. In addition to the classical orders of architecture and instructions in building, this work contains several plates for designs in composition plaster drawn by Daniel Raynerd, a plasterer by training. The plates provided a ready source for other American plasterers who could make molds copied from Raynerd's designs. Through this method Raynerd's work was reproduced by American builders throughout the United States.

The illustrations found in *The American Builder's Companion* are not unlike the plasterwork in the Music Room, reception hall, and long hall of the Baum-Taft House. The museum's Music Room contains a plaster cornice with a delicate motif of grapes and grapevines (fig. 3). The same motif is found in plate 27 of Benjamin and Raynerd's work, where it is recommended for use as the outer band of a ceiling medallion (fig. 4). Both the reception and long halls contain acanthus ceiling medallions with foliated outer bands (figs. 5, 6). Again, these classically derived ornaments have a direct prototype in *The American Builder's Companion*, the most plausible source for a design of this period (fig. 7).

Baum's earliest efforts to sell his "new House" were unsuccessful. The family lived in the house for approximately four years, and on November 12, 1825, Baum deeded the house to the

Fig. 3 Detail, plaster cornice, Music Room, Baum-Taft House. Photography by Anthony Lauro.

Fig. 4 Asher Benjamin and Daniel Raynerd, *The American Builder's Companion*, Boston, 1806, pl. 27, "Fragments for Ceilings."

Fig. 5 Plaster ceiling medallion, long hall, Baum-Taft House. Photography by Anthony Lauro.

Fig. 6 Plaster ceiling medallion, entrance hall, Baum-Taft House. Photography by Anthony Lauro.

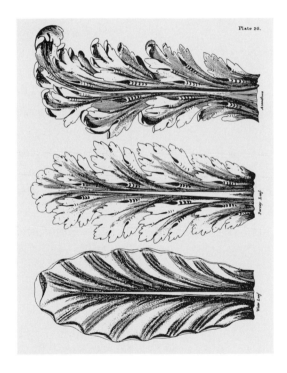

Fig. 7 Asher Benjamin and Daniel Raynerd, *The American Builder's Companion*, Boston, 1806, pl. 26.

Bank of the United States along with a four-and-one-half-acre tract of land.[15] The bank held the property for a short period, during which it was used as a female academy. On September 10, 1829, the house was purchased by the wealthy Cincinnati businessman Nicholas Longworth, with whom it would be associated over the next thirty years.[16] During this time Longworth made changes to the house that constitute an important chapter in the structure's architectural history.

Leading Manufacturers and Merchants asserted that Longworth "finished" the house.[17] Martin Baum's distressing financial state favors this argument, for his initial architectural plans

Fig. 8 Detail, juncture of wing and central section, Baum-Taft House.

Fig. 9 Pike Street elevation, Baum-Taft House, from *Harper's Weekly* (July 1858).

had been severely curtailed by the panic of 1820, and a wealthy new owner would have had to complete the building program. Various pieces of physical evidence suggest that Longworth may have added the two side wings sometime around the 1830s, shortly after he acquired the residence. The wings are somewhat awkwardly connected to the main block (fig. 8); the windows in the wings and the main block are of different sizes and are not aligned; and the treatment of the interior trim differs from one section of the house to the other.

Surviving images document other changes that Longworth made to the main structure, such as the addition of a large fanlight and complementing sidelights. These architectural enhancements of the main doorway do not appear in the 1857 lithograph of the house included in the *Memorial of the Golden Wedding of Nicholas and Susan Longworth Celebrated at Cincinnati on Christmas Eve, 1857* (see fig. 1). Yet they do appear in an illustration published in *Harper's Weekly* in July of the following year, indicating that they were added within that short period (fig. 9). A photograph from around 1925 of the hall interior shows Italianate door trim and the double front doors (fig. 10); it also reveals other major changes. When Longworth renovated the main entrance, he replaced what were apparently the original Baum mantels with Italianate ones of white marble. These fireplace surrounds appear in another photograph taken about 1925 of the Music Room and were probably installed by Longworth in the other principal rooms as well (fig. 11).

The photograph of the Music Room shows another Longworth alteration. The entrance from the hall into the Music Room has a round arched opening that may also date to the 1850s renovation. The ghosts of other presumed original openings are also visible in the hall under the Robert Scott Duncanson murals added by Longworth in the early 1850s. Such changes to doorways improved circulation through the house and may have been a consequence of Longworth's addition of the wings in the 1830s.

Nicholas Longworth died in 1863, and in 1866 the house was leased by his estate to Francis E. Suire.[18] In 1871, after a brief residency, Suire transferred title of the property to David Sinton, a Cincinnati industrialist.[19] Sinton's occupancy of the house was first documented by

Fig. 10 Entrance hall, Baum-Taft House, ca. 1925.

Fig. 11 Music Room, Baum-Taft House, ca. 1925.

A. O. Elzner in a "Sketch of Sinton Residence" of 1882 (fig. 12). The romantic sketch shows a comfortable-looking structure partially covered by overgrown vegetation; awnings shelter the windows on the north wing. The sketch is typical of drawings made during this period of "old-fashioned" residences considered to be of local historic interest. David Sinton's occupation of the house is overshadowed by the renown of his daughter, Anna, and son-in-law, Charles Phelps Taft. The couple were, in fact, married in the Music Room on December 4, 1873,[20] and continued to live in the house until their respective deaths in 1931 and 1929. David Sinton also resided there until his death in 1900.[21]

The Sintons and Tafts further altered the appearance of the house, reflecting the eclecticism of the architectural fashions of the time. Photographic and written documentation attests

Fig. 12 A. O. Elzner, "Sketch of Sinton Residence," 1882, Cincinnati.

to the owners' extremely high aspirations to transform their dwelling into a showcase for one of America's finest private art collections. It should be emphasized that the major alterations involved in the Sinton-Taft treatment of the house were, for the most part, executed in a sensitive manner. When David Sinton acquired the house, it was fifty years old. Changes made by Longworth had already stylishly updated the house, and both Sinton and the Tafts were content to live with those changes. Longworth's alterations continued to appear in photographs as late as about 1925, complemented by the subsequent Sinton-Taft alterations.

David Sinton most significantly changed the house by enlarging it. He added the north bedroom wing, which first appeared on the *Insurance Maps of Cincinnati* in 1891 (fig. 13).[22] A porte-cochère was presumably added at the same time but does not appear on the map (fig. 14). In addition, the Sinton-Taft occupancy also witnessed important stylistic changes that merit closer attention.

Charles Frederick Goss made the following observation on the Tafts and their residence in his monumental work, *Cincinnati, the Queen City:* "The house neither in its architecture, furnishings, nor decoration makes any pretence to any particular style, nor is there any trace of that wretched thing so incompatible with the sense of home, the trail of the collector. Yet the architecture is predominately colonial." Goss became more specific when he noted the Taft improvements: "There is a sense of great wealth spent lavishly but quietly for comfort and beauty. There is perfect harmony. . . . The woodwork furnishings of the library are wonderful black Flemish oak carvings."[23] Goss's commentary is significant for a number of reasons. Since he was a contemporary and social equal of the Tafts, his statement may be considered to reflect the sentiments of the Tafts' social and intellectual peers. Implicit in Goss's writing are a number of issues. The Tafts, for example, lived in an architecturally eclectic house, the product of changes made by a previous owner as well as those made during their own residence. Although the styles were mixed, the house maintained its "colonial" character and therefore was a landmark from an earlier period of Cincinnati's architectural history. Through their wealth, the Tafts were able to embellish it in a tasteful manner.

Goss singled out for commentary the library and its "wonderful black Flemish oak carvings." Photographs taken about 1925 show an extraordinary space that reflects Goss's assessment of "wealth spent lavishly but quietly for comfort and beauty." The Tafts' library is an

Fig. 13 Detail, *Insurance Maps of 1891, Cincinnati, Ohio,* central map, Chicago. Survey & Publishing Company, pp. 11–12. Courtesy of the Cincinnati Historical Society.

Fig. 14 North elevation, Baum-Taft House, 1890s.

exuberant expression of the American aesthetic period, which can be favorably compared with other spaces illustrated in *Artistic Houses,* a compendium of American domestic interiors published in 1883–84. Indeed, the quality of the woodcarving in the Taft library is equal to any found in *Artistic Houses* and merits consideration within Cincinnati's architectural history.

The history of wood carving in Cincinnati has received a great deal of attention, especially in its late-nineteenth-century manifestations.[24] An earlier occupant of the Baum-Taft House helped to bring artistic wood carving to Cincinnati: Joseph Longworth, son of Nicholas, invited the British immigrant wood-carvers Henry and William Fry to Cincinnati to decorate his mansion, Rookwood. The two noted wood-carvers virtually established the art form in Cincinnati with their work on the residence of Joseph's daughter, Maria Longworth Nichols, and her husband, George Ward Nichols. Eventually, Henry Fry, together with Benn Pitman, another British immigrant, was an instructor in wood carving at the University of Cincinnati School of Design.[25] Interest in wood carving soon spread. Cincinnati's citizens produced many notable expressions of the craft during the American aesthetic movement, with Benn Pitman's own house (1883–90) being the quintessential architectural masterpiece.

Could the library woodwork have been executed during the ownership of Joseph Longworth, well before the Frys and Pitman practiced their craft in Cincinnati? This is unlikely, since the "wonderful black Flemish oak carvings" were not popular during the time either Nicholas or Joseph Longworth owned the house. Rather, the state of the room in the photograph of about 1925 reflects the Sinton-Taft period and deserves consideration within that context.

The library had several salient architectural features. In a photograph of the room looking northwest, a doorway leading into the main entrance hall has a fully carved, gadrooned entablature supported by fluted columns with ornately carved capitals resting on richly foliated

Fig. 15 Northwest view, library, Baum-Taft House, ca. 1925.

balusters positioned on plinths (fig. 15). The doorway is flanked by bookcases topped with carved pediments decorated with enlarged gadrooning, akin to that of the doorway pediment. A similar doorway pediment appears in a photograph looking to the southeast of the room (fig. 16). Unfortunately, this doorway is obscured by a painting on an easel, so it cannot be studied in its entirety. However, the mantel and overmantel are visible and merit attention.

The mantel is very richly carved and consists of an elaborately executed frieze flanked by zoomorphic consoles supporting a mantel shelf, which is topped by an overmantel with a carved pediment. The base of the pediment exhibits the same gadrooned treatment as the door heads, suggesting that the doorways, mantels, and bookcases were conceived for the room at the same time and were intended to work as an ensemble. Goss's descriptive phrase, "Flemish oak carvings," suggests that their stylistic source of inspiration was sixteenth-century Flemish woodwork. Unfortunately, the creator of the architectural carving is not known, and all the carvings were removed and destroyed during the 1930s when the house became the Taft Museum.

In 1910 the Cincinnati architectural firm of Elzner and Anderson renovated the Tafts' dining room. The remodeling called for enlarging an existing room and creating a small breakfast nook. The resulting dining-breakfast room became a chaste neoclassical statement (fig. 17). An ornamental plasterwork ceiling was installed in the dining room, its design inspired by the work of the eighteenth-century British architects Robert and James Adam. The newly created breakfast room was separated from the main dining room by a pair of columns, a treatment

Fig. 16 Southeast view, library, Baum-Taft House, ca. 1925.

Fig. 17 Dining room, Baum-Taft House, ca. 1925.

also derived from the work of the Adam brothers. Chippendale- and Hepplewhite-style furniture was chosen to complement the architecture, since this style of furniture was typical of what was then found in a Georgian-revival dining room.

In 1917 Elzner and Anderson also drew plans for a two-story picture gallery, which the Tafts never executed (figs. 18a, b). It is not known whether the firm was also responsible for the neoclassical plasterwork that ornamented the walls of the Music Room (fig. 19). Adamesque in its inspiration, the plasterwork served as a complement to the early-nineteenth-century composition-plaster decoration. The firm may also have been responsible, at least in part, for the installation of parquetry flooring, which replaced the original pine boards (fig. 20). A. O. Elzner had sketched the house as early as 1882, suggesting that he had been involved with other Sinton-Taft renovations well before the dining-room commission of 1910.

The role of the Baum-Taft House as a private dwelling ended with Anna Taft's death in 1931. According to the Tafts' deed of gift, the residence became a public museum, administered by the Cincinnati Institute of Fine Arts.[26] When first opened to the public as the Taft Museum in 1932, the Baum-Taft House had undergone a substantial architectural renovation. Again, the changes need to be considered within the context of Cincinnati in the 1930s. Fortunately, much written and pictorial documentation survives.

The philosophical basis of the 1930s architectural remodeling can be found in the *Bulletin of the Cincinnati Art Museum* for January 1933, in an article written by Walter Siple, the director of the Cincinnati Art Museum and the Taft Museum's first director. Siple wrote:

> An effort was made to restore the interior as nearly as possible to its original appearance. . . . Our idea with regard to the installation was to provide a dignified background for the Taft collections—this background to reflect the feelings of a home of the first quarter of the nineteenth century. . . . It is surprising how successfully the architecture of the early republic lends itself to the exhibition of the collection. There is an abstract unity derived from classical ideals in this period which does not force itself upon the spectator.[27]

A key word in Siple's statement is "restore." It was the intention of the Cincinnati Institute of Fine Arts, in collaboration with the Cincinnati architectural firm of Garber & Woodward, to "restore" the house to its condition in "the first quarter of the nineteenth century," the period when Martin Baum erected the house. Thus, the house would have to undergo specific

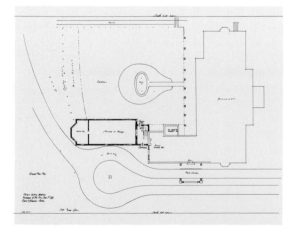
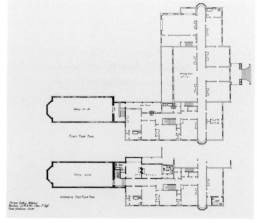

Fig. 18 Elzner and Anderson, "Picture Gallery Additions, Residence of Mr. & Mrs. Charles P. Taft."

Fig. 19 South view, Music Room, Baum-Taft House, ca. 1925.

Fig. 20 North view, Music Room, Baum-Taft House, ca. 1925.

changes to achieve the objective of the restorers. Architectural members that were not within the parameters of the restoration period would have to be removed. Siple justified this facet of the project by stating that the purpose of the restoration was "to provide a dignified background for the Taft collections." Did that mean that the Taft House—as it was occupied by the Tafts—was not dignified?

The restorers confronted the fact that the Taft collection—the reason for the Taft Museum—had always been displayed in a residential context. Like any residence over one hundred years old, the house had become eclectic. This stylistic evolution did not bother the Tafts, who not only lived comfortably in the old house but also added their own improvements. The fact that the house contained Martin Baum's woodwork and plasterwork, Longworth's mantels, and the Tafts' Flemish woodwork obviously troubled the restorers. They decided to restore the house to one period, its first, thereby eliminating the supposed architectural distractions.

Numerous sources indicated that the house had been altered. In 1904 Charles Theodore Greve wrote in the *Centennial History of Cincinnati:* "The door, where the character of a house is so strongly told, has suffered a base 'alteration' and no longer holds the half-wheeled transoms that once must have been the greatest ornament of the house."[28] Even Fiske Kimball, while discussing the house as a landmark, observed: "The original doorway, to be sure, was replaced by one of Victorian pattern, and the lamps with their heavy pedestals mere additions of the period."[29] If restored to its original appearance, all such distractions, interior and exterior, would have to be eliminated.

In 1933, when Siple wrote his article, a precedent existed in the United States for complete and uncompromising architectural restoration, demonstrated by the Rockefeller restoration of Colonial Williamsburg, begun in the late 1920s. John D. Rockefeller and his associates not only "restored" Colonial Williamsburg, they re-created it, removing nineteenth-century buildings and completely rebuilding eighteenth-century ones, sometimes with salvaged earlier architectural components, sometimes with new materials. The same method was followed in the restoration of the Taft Museum.

The main doorway provides a case study of the restoration. As constructed in the 1930s, it consists of a handsome double-door entrance with a large fanlight and accompanying side-

Fig. 21 Garber & Woodward, "Pike Street Elevation," 1931.

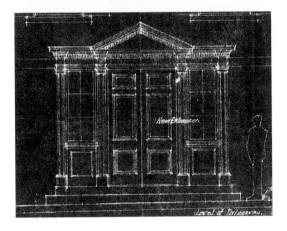

Fig. 22 Garber & Woodward, "New Entrance," Taft Museum, 1931.

lights, the prototypical federal-style doorway (fig. 21). Yet there is no historical basis for the doorway's form, since the earliest known depiction of the house, the 1857 lithograph, shows neither fanlight nor sidelights (see fig. 1). Three drawings in the museum archives for the north entrance of the house depict viable candidates for the Pike Street entrance, yet all three are conjectural and not based on historical evidence (figs. 22a, b, c). Indeed, such an elaborate side entrance would have been most unlikely in Martin Baum's Cincinnati, so that selecting any one of the three becomes a matter of taste. The third drawing was ultimately chosen.

In "restoring" the interior mantels, the architects followed the Williamsburg model of replacing features with period materials. The mantels were salvaged from local residences and are vernacular expressions of the Adamesque style (fig. 23). While such mantels are in keeping with the early-nineteenth-century fabric, evidence of the original mantels was never found.

Several aspects of the restoration deviated from the goal of creating a complete early-nineteenth-century residence, the most striking of which was the retention of the Robert S. Duncanson murals. Their preservation is owed primarily to Walter Siple, who had them restored. Trained as an art historian, Siple recognized the historical and artistic value of the works and was willing to rework the Taft collection around them. Siple's view was easily justified, since they were works of art in the house during the Taft occupation and could continue to be treated as part of the Taft collection.

The display of small objects also resulted in a restoration compromise. Although the Tafts lived freely with smaller objects from their collection, the fact that the museum would be open

Fig. 23 Fireplace mantel, Taft Museum.

Fig. 24 Display cases, President's Room, Taft Museum.

to the public precluded such an approach. Display cases were needed to house and protect them, and Garber & Woodward designed cases that combined neoclassical detail with contemporary art deco features (fig. 24). This sense of 1930s design spills over in certain rooms into the trim, providing a marked contrast to the early-nineteenth-century detail that survives throughout the house.

The Taft Museum opened to the public on November 29, 1932. Since the time that Walter Siple wrote his article on the Taft Museum's renovation, much has changed both in the philosophy of architectural restoration and in our knowledge of Martin Baum's building period. The fields of architectural history and restoration have changed to the extent that the kinds of decisions that Walter Siple made on the basis of aesthetics may now be determined through a combination of scientific and architectural analysis.

Over a half century after its opening, the Taft Museum is itself a "period" piece, its interior and exterior reflecting the past occupations of the Baum, Longworth, Sinton, and Taft families (figs. 25, 26). Beneath the accumulated layers of paint, wood, and plaster lies more material evidence of these past occupations. Time will determine the disposition of the Taft Museum's "buried" treasure.

Notes

1. Marilyn Ott, "Martin Baum," unpublished paper, Taft Museum In-School Program, Mar. 1975, with a bibliography added in 1977, p. 1. Information on Baum is extracted from this source. See also Jayne Merkel, "The Baum-Taft House: A Historiography," *The Taft Museum: A Cincinnati Legacy*, Cincinnati, 1988, pp. 33–50.

2. Ott, p. 1.

3. Daniel Symmes to Martin Baum, Sept. 1, 1812, Deed Book S, p. 284, Hamilton County, Ohio.

4. Ott, p. 4.

5. Letter from Martin Baum to William Lytle, Aug. 22, 1820, William Lytle Papers, Cincinnati Historical Society.

6. "By a Citizen," *The Cincinnati Directory*, Cincinnati, 1819, pp. 32, 33.

7. *Historical Places and Landmarks: Leading Manufacturers and Merchants of Cincinnati and Environs*, New York, 1886, p. 37.

8. *Leading Manufacturers*, p. 37.

9. *Inland Architect and News Record*, vol. x (Nov. 1887), no. 70 and p. 1.

10. Montgomery Schuyler, *Architectural Record*, vol. XXIII (1908), pp. 341–46.

11. Fiske Kimball, "Masterpieces of Early American Art," Art and Archaeology (Sept.–Oct. 1919), p. 297.

12. I. T. Frary, *Early Homes of Ohio*, 1st ed., 1936, New York, 1970, p. 155.

13. *Cincinnati Directory*, pp. 49, 50.

Fig. 25 Music Room, Taft Museum.

14. Robert Wellford, "To the Public," advertisement, Stauffer Collection, Historical Society of Pennsylvania, Philadelphia.

15. Martin Baum to the Bank of the United States, Nov. 12, 1825, Deed Book 24, p. 618, Hamilton County, Ohio.

16. Bank of the United States to Nicholas Longworth, Sept. 10, 1829, Deed Book 34, p. 34, Hamilton County, Ohio.

17. *Leading Manufacturers*, p. 37.

18. Nicholas Longworth per Executors to Francis E. Suire, June 4, 1866, Lease Book 29, p. 166, Hamilton County, Ohio.

19. Francis E. Suire and wife to David Sinton, Oct. 10, 1871, Deed Book 393, p. 292, Hamilton County, Ohio.

20. *Cincinnati Enquirer*, Dec. 5, 1873.

21. Charles Theodore Greve, *Centennial History of Cincinnati*, vol. II, Chicago, 1904, pp. 170–73.

22. *Insurance Maps of 1891, Cincinnati, Ohio*, vol. I, Chicago, 1891, pp. 11–12.

23. Charles Frederick Goss, *Cincinnati, the Queen City, 1788–1912*, vol. I, Chicago and Cincinnati, 1912, p. 444.

24. Roger B. Stein, "Artifact as Ideology: The Aesthetic Movement in Its American Cultural Context," in *In Pursuit of Beauty: Americans and the Aesthetic Movement*, exh. cat., Metropolitan Museum of Art, New York, 1986, pp. 32–36.

25. Stein, p. 32.

26. Walter Siple, *The Taft Museum*, brochure reprinted from an article in *Bulletin of the Cincinnati Art Museum*, vol. IV, no. 1 (Jan. 1933), pp. 2–3.

27. Siple, pp. 14–15.

28. Greve, vol. I, p. 579.

29. Kimball, p. 297.

Fig. 26 Pike Street façade, Taft Museum.

The Robert S. Duncanson Murals at the Taft Museum

Joseph D. Ketner

The Taft Museum houses one of the most distinctive and significant examples of early-American domestic mural decoration: the Belmont murals by Robert S. Duncanson. Eight large landscape decorations in trompe l'oeil French rococo frames fill the walls of the main entrance and transverse halls. Three over-door decorations of floral bouquets and two of perched eagles complete the decorative ensemble (figs. 1, 2). The Belmont murals mark the boundaries of three traditions in early American culture: wallpaper fashions, domestic mural painting, and the art of landscape painting.

The Taft and Longworth family traditions claim that Nicholas Longworth commissioned the hall murals about 1850 from the regional painter Robert Duncanson. The works are unsigned, and no contemporary records of the murals exist. They are not mentioned by contemporary writers. Longworth did not refer to them in his letters, and the lavish descriptions of the house written for the celebration of the Longworths' golden wedding anniversary in 1857 do not describe them.[1] In the 1939 biography of her great-grandfather, Comtesse Clara Longworth DeChambrun alludes to letters by Nicholas Longworth that cite the author of the murals as "the well-known decorative painter Duncanson."[2] Unfortunately, these papers have been lost for the past fifty years. Despite the lack of contemporary documentation, both oral history and connoisseurship have firmly attributed the works to Duncanson.[3]

The history of the murals is intricately intertwined with that of the house. Construction was under way on this federal-style structure in 1820 for the original owner, Martin Baum. Longworth purchased the grand residence in 1829 to house his growing family and estate.[4] "I have bought 'Belmont' which is large enough to contain all the Longworth's in the nation."[5] Twenty years passed before Longworth commissioned the mural decorations for his front hallways to accompany his collections of paintings, sculptures, and decorative arts. The house with the murals served the family for another decade but was too large after several children married and moved away and after Longworth himself died in 1863.

By the time Longworth's son Joseph sold the house in 1869 to David Sinton, the murals were covered with wallpaper, a change that had taken place within Duncanson's own lifetime.[6] During

Fig. 1 Entrance hall, Taft Museum.

Fig. 2 Transverse hall, Taft Museum.

the late nineteenth century, pattern wallpapers from England were very popular in America, and many layers covered the murals for more than sixty years. Only in 1927, upon the donation of their house to the city of Cincinnati, did Mrs. Charles Phelps Taft mention that mural decorations, which she had never seen, were under the wallpaper in the entrance halls. She remembered hearing her father, David Sinton, discussing the decorations when talking about the history of the house.[7] Upon the transfer of the estate to the city in 1931, Walter Siple, then director of the Cincinnati Art Museum, had the paper removed and made an exciting rediscovery in American art.

The murals were in excellent condition, having been heavily varnished and covered with several layers of wallpaper and paste, which helped to preserve them. Repairing the landscapes required only minor inpainting, particularly to the skies in several panels. With the exception of the floral vignettes over the door to the Music Room, none of the essential elements of the designs was lost (fig. 3). With the restoration complete, the building was opened to the public on November 29, 1932, and the murals were received with enthusiasm.

The sequence of landscape murals and overdoor decorations is a well-orchestrated decorative scheme. A pair of idyllic landscapes flank the entryway. The scenes proceeding down the front hall and through the cross hall become increasingly picturesque and reminiscent of the Ohio River valley. The style of the landscapes falls squarely within the Hudson River School tradition. Unlike many mural cycles, no specific subject or narrative seems to link the panels of the Belmont murals. Although some of the murals allude to the stream or voyage of life, that theme is not conveyed in all the decorations. The motif of a river flowing through the stages of life was popular in romantic landscape painting, as is shown in Thomas Cole's series *The Voyage of Life* (1842, Washington, D.C., National Gallery of Art), which was in Cincinnati during Duncanson's lifetime.[8] The views for the Belmont murals may have been chosen simply to satisfy Longworth's appreciation for both European and regional landscapes. Longworth owned great tracts of land, and some of the scenes may represent actual sites in the Ohio River valley. However, none of Duncanson's sketches or studies survives, so it is impossible to link the murals to specific locations.

Landscapes and floral bouquets bordered with trompe l'oeil frames were very popular in mid-nineteenth-century America. The scheme derives from French wallpaper designs, which were then available in abundance throughout the United States.[9] Duncanson seems to have used a variation on the framing motif found in Etienne Delicourt's pattern book of wallpaper designs from about 1850 (fig. 4).[10] These so-called fresco papers bordered a variety of wallpaper patterns—including figural, floral, and scenic papers—and were widely used at midcentury. It is obvious from photographs of the restoration that a pedestal motif, similar to the wallpaper pattern, was originally used below the wainscoting.

Although French scenic papers were popular in the United States during Duncanson's time, English papers had been in favor earlier.[11] The Belmont murals display influences from both sources. The decoration of the Stephan van Rensselaer home,

Fig. 3 Belmont murals during restoration (1931–32), entrance hall, north wall. Taft Museum.

formerly in Albany, New York, demonstrates the English use of landscape vignettes in wallpaper designs about 1768 (fig. 5). The framing motif has a rococo flamboyance, which was considerably tamed in the frames of the Belmont murals. The English wallpaper vignettes were printed in grisaille to present the illu-

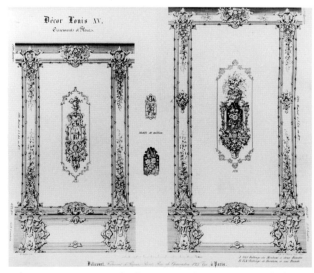

Fig. 4 Plate, Delicourt et Cie, *Décor Louis XV: Ornaments et fleurs*, in *Collection d'esquisses de décoration exécutés en papier peint*, Paris, ca. 1850. Engraving. New York, Smithsonian Institution Libraries, Cooper-Hewitt Branch, courtesy of Art Resource.

Fig. 5 *View from Mont Ferrat, Sardinia,* from an engraving by Jean-Jacques Le Veau after a painting by Joseph Vernet. Wallpaper printed in grisaille on yellow ground. Formerly in great hall, Van Rensselaer Manor House, Albany, New York. New York, The Metropolitan Museum of Art, Gift of Dr. Howard Van Rensselaer, 1928. 28.224.

Fig. 6 Henry Price, lower hall mural, after Joseph DuFour's *Les Voyages du Captain Cook* (1831). Oil on plaster, Carroll House, formerly in Springfield, N.Y. Winterthur, Del., Henry du Pont Winterthur Museum.

sion of reproductive prints, framed and hanging on the wall. Only after 1800 did the French develop the first full-color, continuous landscape views in imitation of paintings. Through the first half of the nineteenth century, French scenic papers were the most sought after. The most prevalent scenes were views of Italy and France; however, some views of America were available. The French panoramic papers created the illusion of a continuous space beyond the wall. The Belmont murals, on the other hand, stress the verticality of the walls and mimic framed paintings. It seems that Duncanson used no one existing wallpaper as an exact source for his murals.

In addition to wallpaper designs, the Belmont murals are also closely related to domestic mural painting, but they are far superior to any examples from before the Civil War. Domestic mural painting in America was the domain of the itinerant painter. Advertising himself as a painter and glazier, the house painter was capable of painting a house, decorating it with murals, painting a coat of arms, gilding, lettering, and coach and sign painting. A patron's likeness could be taken, if so desired. The execution of these works was often crude, because most of the artisans had been apprenticed in the house-painting trade and had no fine-arts training. When executing interior decorations (fig. 6), house painters commonly imitated wallpaper.[12] Duncanson's landscape murals for Nicholas Longworth are no exception. Ironically, Duncanson's murals, which were painted imitations of wallpaper mimicking paintings, were eventually covered by the wallpaper they were created to imitate.

1. A review of the contemporary Cincinnati newspapers (the *Gazette* and *Enquirer*), Nicholas Longworth's letters in the Cincinnati Historical Society, and the *Golden Wedding Anniversary* pamphlet and scrapbook (1857) reveals no mention of the decorative mural scheme.

2. Clara Longworth DeChambrun, *Cincinnati: The Story of the Queen City,* New York, 1939, p. 113.

3. Since their discovery the murals have been attributed to no other artist. See Walter Siple, "The Taft Museum," *Bulletin of the Cincinnati Art Museum,* vol. IV, no. 1 (Jan. 1933), pp. 1–21; James A. Porter, "Robert S. Duncanson: Midwestern Romantic-Realist," *Art in America,* vol. XXXIX, no. 3 (Oct. 1951), pp. 99–154; Guy McElroy, *Robert S. Duncanson: A Centennial Exhibition,* exh. cat., Cincinnati Art Museum, 1972. A survey of the DeChambrun family archives, Paris, did not uncover the letters mentioned by the comtesse, and they remain lost.

4. Siple, pp. 3–5.

5. Clara Longworth DeChambrun, *The Making of Nicholas Longworth,* New York, 1933, p. 39.

6. Siple, p. 4.

7. Siple, p. 7, and Ruth Neely, "Art Treasures of Old Taft Home," *Cincinnati Post,* Nov. 29, 1932, p. 1.

8. Anthony Janson, "The Cincinnati Landscape Tradition," *Celebrate Cincinnati Art,* exh. cat., Cincinnati Art Museum, 1982, p. 13.

9. Catherine Lynn, *Wallpaper in America: From the Seventeenth Century to World War I,* New York, 1980, p. 228.

10. Catherine Lynn Frangiamore, *Wallpaper in Historic Preservation,* Washington, D.C., 1977, p. 33.

11. Lynn, p. 89.

12. Nina Fletcher Little, *American Decorative Wall Painting, 1700–1850,* New York, 1972, pp. xix, 85.

Robert S. Duncanson

Fayette, New York 1821–1872 Detroit

Duncanson was a self-taught, second-generation artist in the Hudson River School style. Born in 1821 in Fayette, New York, to a mulatto family of handymen and house painters, he moved with his family to Monroe, Michigan, around 1832.[1] Here Duncanson apprenticed as a house painter and, for approximately one year, he and an associate, James Gamblin, worked in Monroe as painters and glaziers.[2] The two disbanded around 1840, and young Duncanson moved to Cincinnati to embark on a career as an independent artist. During the 1840s he worked as an itinerant artist, moving regularly among Cincinnati, Monroe, and Detroit. He copied prints and painted portraits and estate views; his painting ultimately attracted the attention of Nicholas Longworth.

A major landholder and horticulturist, Longworth had a reputation for sponsoring artists he felt had both great merit and great need. In his correspondence to the sculptor Hiram Powers, Longworth wrote often about the arts in Cincinnati and mentioned Duncanson on several occasions. In one letter Longworth remarked, "One of our most promising painters is a light mulatto by the name of Duncanson. He is a man of great industry and worth."[3] The respect Longworth held for Duncanson was manifest in the commission to decorate the entrance halls of his home, Belmont. That Duncanson had created nothing of this scale and complexity before demonstrates Longworth's confidence in the young artist. Having begun his career as a painter and glazier, Duncanson was already familiar with interior decoration and wallpaper fashions. However, such a mural commission was remarkable for an artist in his formative stages, and the fact that Duncanson created no subsequent work on this scale establishes the murals as his most ambitious achievement.

Although Duncanson's work had matured slowly during the 1840s, his artistic ability increased dramatically in the 1850s. In 1850 Duncanson moved into a studio adjoining that of William Sonntag, the foremost landscape painter west of the Appalachian Mountains, on Fourth Street in Cincinnati.[4] From Sonntag, Duncanson learned many painting techniques, and his works began to reflect Sonntag's style, an Ohio River valley variation on the Hudson River School style. As the records for exhibitions in Cincinnati for the 1850s show, under Sonntag's influence Duncanson also began to produce primarily landscape paintings. It was during this period that Duncanson created the Belmont murals. Sonntag's influence and the challenge of creating the Belmont murals forced Duncanson into artistic maturity and launched his career of critical and popular success in the United States, Canada, and England during the 1850s and 1860s. Coming at a crucial period in his artistic development, these two factors allowed him to become the first African-American artist to earn a national and international reputation as a landscape painter.

1. United States Census: New York State, Seneca County, Fayette (1830), p. 66; Michigan, Monroe County, Monroe (1840), p. 6. Dennis Au, assistant director of the Monroe County Historical Museum, who discovered Duncanson's Monroe connection, believes the family arrived there around 1832. See also James E. DeVries, *Race and Kinship in a Midwestern Town*, Chicago, 1984, p. 14.

2. *Monroe Gazette* [Mich.], Apr. 17, 1838–Apr. 9, 1839.

3. Letter from Nicholas Longworth to Hiram Powers, June 20, 1852, Cincinnati Historical Society.

4. *Cincinnati Daily Gazette*, Jan. 30, 1850.

Eagle Vignettes

1820s–40s

Oil on plaster: 1932.242, 83.8 x 204.2 cm (33 x 80⅜ in.); 1932.243, 83.2 x 202.6 cm (32¾ x 79¾ in.)

The two eagle vignettes above the arched doorways in the transverse hall of the Taft Museum appear to be the earliest of the mural decorations. The style differs greatly from Duncanson's work. Although his early painting *The Vulture and Its Prey* (1844) displays a similarly crude understanding of avian anatomy, especially obvious where the neck joins the head to the body (fig. 1), the flat tan background and the frames of the two vignettes are completely unlike the rest of the mural scheme. If the eagles were part of the mural commission, Duncanson probably would have used a background similar to that of the floral vignettes or a color in the tonal range of the rest of the scheme.

Fig. 1 Robert S. Duncanson, *Vulture and Its Prey*, 1844. Oil on canvas, 68.9 x 56.5 cm (27⅛ x 22¼ in.). Washington, D.C., National Museum of American Art, Smithsonian Institution, gift of Harold E. Deal. 1983.95.163.

1932.243

Instead, the eagle vignettes more closely resemble the work typical of late-eighteenth-century itinerant house painters. Such images were popular in the decades following the American Revolution but occur less frequently during the nineteenth century.[1] Therefore, another artist very likely painted these vignettes in an early style after the construction of the house in 1820 but before Duncanson's murals of 1850–52.

1. Nina Fletcher Little, *American Decorative Wall Painting, 1700–1850*, New York, 1972, p. 49.

Literature *Catalogue of the Taft Museum*, Cincinnati, 1939 and 1958, nos. 486, 501; Joseph D. Ketner II, "The Belmont Murals in the Taft Museum," *The Taft Museum: A Cincinnati Legacy*, Cincinnati, 1988, pp. 56–57 (ill.).

1932.242, 1932.243

Robert S. Duncanson

Floral Vignettes

1850–52
Oil on plaster: 1932.244, 78.4 x 150.5 cm (30⅞ x 59¼ in.); 1932.245, 75.9 x 147.3 cm (29⅞ x 58 in.); 1932.246, 80.6 x 185.4 cm (31¾ x 73 in.)

The floral bouquets over the doorways in the transverse hall of the Taft Museum are closely related to French wallpaper styles. Bouquets by designers such as Jean Zuber were frequently in-

corporated into framed vertical panels or overmantel decorations (fig. 1). American wallpaper manufacturers often imitated this French design, which was frequently used to decorate fireboards.[1] One design at Old Sturbridge Village, Massachusetts, provides the general prototype for the floral vignettes in the

Fig. 1 Jean Zuber, *Floral Bouquet*, ca. 1800. Block-printed wallpaper. Paris, Bibliothèque Nationale.

1932.244

Fig. 2 *Floral Fireboard*, ca. 1800–1810. French block-printed wallpaper mounted on canvas. Old Sturbridge Village, Mass. Photography by Henry E. Peach.

and a single floral vignette was painted in by the conservators over the entrance to the Music Room.

1. Catherine Lynn, *Wallpaper in America: From the Seventeenth Century to World War I*, New York, 1980, pp. 250–51.

2. Nina Fletcher Little, *American Decorative Wall Painting, 1700–1850*, New York, 1972, p. 66.

Literature *Catalogue of the Taft Museum*, Cincinnati, 1939 and 1958, nos. 491, 496; Joseph D. Ketner II, "The Belmont Murals in the Taft Museum," *The Taft Museum: A Cincinnati Legacy*, Cincinnati, 1988, pp. 55–56 (ill).

1932.244–46

Belmont mural scheme (fig. 2) and is directly linked with the fashions of American domestic mural painters. Such designs were also the standard for itinerant house painters and, like the wallpapers, were usually found over mantels and on fireboards and less often over entryways and doors, as in the Belmont murals.[2]

Unfortunately, the floral vignette over the Music Room door had to be entirely repainted and must now be judged to be the work of a restorer (fig. 3). Originally, three vignettes decorated a much larger doorway to the Music Room. Because only portions of those vignettes remained when the wallpaper was removed, they were covered with house paint during restoration,

Fig. 3 Belmont murals during restoration (1931–32), transverse hall, east wall. Taft Museum.

☙

Robert S. Duncanson

Eight Landscape Murals

1850–52
Oil on plaster, dimensions in text

Although the murals decorating the transverse and entrance halls of the Taft Museum are not firmly dated, a comparison with Duncanson's easel paintings would date the mural commission to between 1850 and 1852. Such a comparison also allows one to consider the sequence in which the artist may have executed the murals. In general, the murals in the transverse hall recall Duncanson's work of the 1840s, while the work in the entrance hall looks forward to his paintings of the later 1850s, showing the artist's increased skill in draftsmanship, paint handling, and composition. This qualitative progression implies the following sequence for the creation of the landscape murals.

The murals on the east wall of the transverse hall are the least accomplished. On the north side of the Music Room door, Duncanson created one of the wildest landscape views, a dynamic composition of a rugged hill rising out of a ravine (1932.233, 278.8 x 195.6 cm [109¾ x 77 in.]). The tepee in the lower right leads the viewer to a pair of figures gazing at a cascade. The radical incline of a hill is an infrequently used compositional device in landscape painting at this time. Although this is the most original composition among the murals, the

1932.235

tepee and the figures betray the artist's immature drawing style. The weakness of draftsmanship and definition of foliage is characteristic of Duncanson's work of the 1840s, making this one of the earlier murals.

On the south side of the Music Room door, the mural portrays what appears to be a rural Scottish scene with a shepherd grazing his flock in the foreground before a ruined medieval castle (1932.235, 279.7 x 202.3 cm [110⅛ x 79⅝ in.]). The theme of ruins and the fantastic architecture recall the English romantic landscape painting tradition. An early unsigned and undated painting, probably from the late 1840s, typifies Duncanson's use of this compositional formula and these motifs (fig. 1). In the easel painting the medieval structure on the hill overlooks a winding river with a sailboat; the mural repeats this composition. Because of its smaller size, the easel painting is handled in greater detail, an approach unlikely to be used on the large scale of the murals. In this scene Duncanson had difficulty defining the recession of space. His figures, sheep, and architectural details are also weak in comparison to the other murals in the Belmont cycle, suggesting that this panel, too, was executed early in the project.

The panels on the west wall of the transverse hall are considerably more accomplished. On the north side Duncanson has portrayed a family at the door of an English-style cottage nestled in trees (1932.234, 279.4 x 217.8 cm [110 x 85¾ in.]). In the distance stands a group of buildings similar to the warehouses that would have been found on the Cincinnati riverfront at that time.

1932.233

Fig. 1 Robert S. Duncanson, *Scotch Highlands,* ca. 1848–52. Oil on canvas, 69.2 x 107.3 cm (27¼ x 42¼ in.). Washington, D.C., National Museum of American Art, gift of Sol and Lillian Koffler.

1932.234

This domestic scene recalls Duncanson's early *Drunkard's Plight* (1845) in the Detroit Institute of Arts (fig. 2). Although the mural abandons the easel painting's moralizing, melodramatic narrative, the elements of the compositions are the same: in the foreground a cottage with figures in the doorway and a distant landscape view to the left. During the 1780s Thomas Gainsborough introduced and popularized the cottage door theme. Duncanson was certainly familiar with Gainsborough's works from the prints and reproductions that he often studied and copied during the 1840s.

On the southwest side of the transverse hall is a rocky riverscape unique among the murals in its lack of human references (1932.237, 280 x 219.1 cm [110¼ x 86¼ in.]). The focus of the composition is the swiftly flowing river. Surging forth from the distance, the river winds into the foreground, where it cascades into a hidden ravine only to reappear pouring into the spectator's space. It breaks the foreground plane and places the viewer precariously in the middle of the rapids. This dramatic

Fig. 2 Robert S. Duncanson, *The Drunkard's Plight,* 1845. Oil on canvas, 38.7 x 50.2 cm (15¼ x 19¾ in.). The Detroit Institute of Arts, gift of Miss Sarah M. Sheridan, 44.277.

1932.237

Fig. 3 Robert S. Duncanson, *Landscape with Shepherd*, 1852. Oil on canvas, 82.6 x 122.6 cm (32½ x 48¼ in.). New York, The Metropolitan Museum of Art, gift of Hanson K. Corning by exchange, 1975, 1975.88.

1932.241

panel is the first mural in the sequence to anticipate Duncanson's landscapes of the 1850s, particularly *Landscape with Shepherd* of 1852 (fig. 3). The framing trees, cascading falls, and rotting trunks all relate the mural to the later easel painting. This panel is undoubtedly the most accomplished among those in the transverse hall.

In the entrance hall, the northeast mural offers a variation on the compositional format just discussed (1932.241, 276.2 x 222.9 cm [108¾ x 87¾ in.]). This similarity suggests a possible sequence in the execution of the murals from the transverse hall into the entrance hall. Here the river, a torrent in the previous design, gently flows into the foreground and safely off to the left. Two trees sprouting fresh foliage frame the view onto buildings nestled in the rolling hillside. The rocky riverbank is accessible, and a harmonious reverie on nature is evoked. The golden light emanating from the horizon bathes the scene in the idyllic glow of a classical landscape.

The two murals flanking the main entrance of the Taft Museum are also classically inspired pastoral scenes. On the north side, tall stately trees anchor the left side of the panel, while a river winds into the luminous distance on the right (1932.240, 276.9 x 233.1 cm [109 x 91¾ in.]). The grand estate in the middle ground is the focus of the painting and the stage for an anecdotal group of figures boarding a boat. Although Duncanson's buildings and arched bridge are imaginary, the imagery has its source in similar harbor scenes by J. M. W. Turner and ultimately in those by Claude Lorrain. In the guise of an oriental romance, the fantastic architecture and boaters reappear later in Duncanson's two versions of the *Vale of Kashmir* (1864, private collection; 1867, Detroit, private collection). The subject for *Vale of Kashmir* is derived from the popular epic poem *Lalla Rookh* (1817) by the British romantic author Thomas Moore.

The mural on the south side of the front entrance displays the greatest influence from European masters of classical landscape (1932.239, 277.8 x 232.1 cm [109⅜ x 91⅜ in.]). The balanced

1932.240

1932.239

composition stabilizes a quiet scene of horse riders crossing a bridge over a winding river that flows evenly to the luminous horizon. The arched bridges and framing groups of trees are also hallmarks of a classical landscape composition. Having access

Fig. 4 After Joseph M. W. Turner, *Bridge in the Middle Distance*, 1808. From the *Liber Studiorum* (no. 4), etching and mezzotint, plate 18.1 x 26.4 cm (7⅛ x 10⅜ in.). Indianapolis Museum of Art, bequest of Kurt F. Pantzer, Sr.

to the many printed volumes of masterworks circulated among artists, Duncanson was certainly aware of these prototypes. In this case, Turner's *Bridge in the Middle Distance* from the *Liber Studiorum* could have served as a source, as could several other compositions in that portfolio (fig. 4).

The final landscape panel on the southeast wall of the entrance hall is the finest (1932.238, 279.1 x 220.4 cm. [109⅞ x 86¾ in.]). Unlike the other entrance-hall murals, it depicts a wilderness scene with twisting, rotting tree trunks and a swiftly flowing river. Gazing into the rich sunset on the horizon, a group of pioneers rests atop a rocky prominence. The bright hues of the sunset and the highly expressive tree trunks set this panel apart from all the other murals. In addition, the thick textures of the tree bark and the details of the foliage demonstrate markedly improved paint handling on Duncanson's part. The twisting, storm-blasted tree trunks were stock motifs in the repertoires of Hudson River School artists. They appear for the first time in Duncanson's work in these murals.

Although very little documentation exists linking Duncanson to the murals, a comparison with his easel paintings leaves no doubt that they are his work. Despite his having created nothing comparable prior to this commission, Duncanson summoned his great industry and rose to the challenge. By contracting the decoration of his home to a young, untrained artist, Longworth revealed a remarkable trust in Duncanson. The result of that trust and Longworth's philanthropic spirit is the legacy to American art that now graces the halls of the Taft Museum.

Literature Walter Siple, "The Taft Museum," *Bulletin of the Cincinnati Art Museum,* vol. IV, no. 1 (Jan. 1933), pp. 1–21; Clara Longworth DeChambrun, *Cincinnati: The Story of the Queen City,* New York, 1939, p. 113; *Catalogue of the Taft Museum,* Cincinnati, 1939 and 1958, nos. 487, 488, 490, 492, 495, 497, 499, 500; James A. Porter, "Robert S. Duncanson: Midwestern Romantic-Realist," *Art in America,* vol. XXXIX, no. 3 (Oct. 1951), pp. 99–154; Guy McElroy, *Robert S. Duncanson: A Centennial Exhibition,* exh. cat., Cincinnati Art Museum, 1972, pp. 8–9; Joseph D. Ketner II, "Robert S. Duncanson, 1821–1872: The Late Literary Landscape Paintings," *The American Art Journal,* vol. XV, no. 1 (Winter 1983), pp. 41–42, fig. 8 (1932.240); *Nicholas Longworth: Art Patron of Cincinnati,* exh. cat., Taft Museum, 1988, cover ill. (1932.238); Joseph D. Ketner II, "The Belmont Murals in the Taft Museum," *The Taft Museum: A Cincinnati Legacy,* Cincinnati, 1988, pp. 51–63.

1932.233–35 and 1932.237–41

1932.238

Furniture and Interior Decoration at the Taft Museum

Lisa Krieger

INTERIOR design is the most ephemeral of the decorative arts. Exposed to daily wear and tear, at the mercy of the whims of fashion, and usually disbursed every generation, it is far more vulnerable to change than the architecture enclosing it. Thus, it is not surprising that the furniture and furnishings currently installed in the Taft Museum are, in the main, expressions of neither the builder nor the subsequent owners of the Baum-Taft House but rather reflect the vision of Walter P. Siple, the museum's first director. In 1931 it became his responsibility to navigate the transition from private home to public institution, and his choices determined the interpretation of a house that had evolved through the ownership of three affluent families and more than a century of rapidly changing tastes. For Siple the project seems to have been a labor of love, since he approached it with equal measures of scholarly thoroughness and creative enthusiasm.

Siple had few tangible clues to the early history of the house on which to base his decisions. If little information on the design and construction of Martin Baum's house has come to light, far less is known about its original contents. No inventory of the estate has been found, and the surviving mentions of the house during its first period are but vague and few. One early recorded description of Baum's residence dates to 1864, just after his wife's death and thirty-nine years after he sold it, and notes only that "for those days [it was] quite a splendid mansion. When it was finished he gave a party. . . . There were present a large number of the old pioneers (now residing with the dead)."[1] This observation is helpful only to the extent that although the house was considered unfinished when Nicholas Longworth purchased it, it was used for entertaining during the Baum family's short tenure of ownership.[2] Henry Howe further documented this fact in 1888 when he wrote that Baum's "hospitable home was open to all intellectually great men that visited Cincinnati, and German literary men were especially welcome."[3]

With only these meager descriptions and the evidence of the ambitious exterior architecture and interior plasterwork details, we can draw some assumptions about how the house might have looked in 1825 before Baum met with the financial reverses that forced him to sell it to the Bank of the United States on November 12 of that year.[4] Contemporaneous Cincinnati newspapers indicate the sorts of furnishings that would have been available locally. For example, on December 11, 1819, Charles Lehman, a cabinet- and chairmaker from Philadelphia, advertised his "new cabinet Wareroom on Seventh Street, between Main and Sycamore Sts., next door but one east of Watson's Clock Manufactory [where he] will execute his orders in a style of workmanship equal to any west of the mountains." He then adds, "Being well acquainted with the newest and most fashionable patterns of cabinetwork executed in Philadelphia, he feels the most perfect confidence in inviting public patronage."[5]

Most certainly like his neighbor, William Lytle, who furnished his Mansion House in 1815 with goods made locally by Benjamin Porter, Baum would have outfitted his house with the products of Cincinnati's young but burgeoning shops and manufactories.[6] As Jane Sikes explains in her investigation of the early Ohio furniture industry, "We can feel quite positive that into the 1820s Cincinnatians became more dependent on their home manufactories than ever. The 1820 depression had caused merchants (Baum, Kilgour, and others) to realize the importance of buying everything they could locally, in order to keep as much capital in the city as possible."[7] Sikes further notes that before 1830 imported furniture was never advertised in the city.[8]

Other decorative elements were imported by this early date, however, although local manufacturers tried whenever possible to offer a competitive alternative. For instance, in 1820 the firm of Allen and Badger offered "on hand, besides their own make, French papers with borders to match, likewise following landscape views."[9] These imported wallcoverings included the popular series Monuments of Paris, Views of the Banks of the Bosporus, and Cupid and Psyche produced by the renowned French companies of Zuber and Dufour.

If more detailed assumptions about Martin Baum's interiors would be purely speculative, it is clear that even during that early period in the city's history a fair variety of luxury goods in the classical-revival style was available. Items such as mahogany sideboards and tall case clocks, Grecian card tables, and painted and gilt fancy chairs were all being produced locally by the 1820s and, if not on a par with those of the most elegant urban craftsmen such as Duncan Phyfe and Charles-Honoré Lannuier in New York, they were of sufficient style and quality to be appropriate to Baum's new house.

By 1829, when Nicholas Longworth took possession of the house that Baum had built, by then known as Belmont, the choice of goods was expanding. Early in 1830 *The Cincinnati Daily Gazette* offered for sale such up-to-date furniture designs as "pier, dressing, and side tables" (Jan. 19) and "all sorts of Grecian chairs and sofas" (Feb. 11). With the development of the steamboat and the canal system, elegant decorative furnishings of all sorts became even more accessible. Among those advertised in the *Cincinnati Daily Gazette* in 1830 were lighting devices, including "bronze and gilt Grecian lamps with 2, 3 or 4 lights, Bronze chandeliers with figures representing Dance of Canova, alabaster lamps with bronze and gilt chains, candlesticks for pianofortes, and pearl and astral lamps and lampshades." Available floor coverings offered in the *Cincinnati Chronicle* of the same year included Kidderminster, Brussels, and English and Scottish ingrain carpeting as well as "Venetian" stair and passage runners, painted unseamed floorcloths, and, on September 25, "100 assorted rugs." Mantel, pier, and toilette looking glasses, bronze and gilt clocks, all manner of fireplace equipment, sculptures including figures of Napoléon and groups of the gods, and vases of alabaster, "etruscan agate with Raphael ornaments," and yellow sienna marble were other fashionable accessories available for purchase that year.

As is the case with Baum, no inventory of Longworth's household contents is known. His architectural additions and modifications demonstrate, however, that he followed current tastes during the nearly four decades he lived in the house. Those years saw the neoclassicism of the early federal period evolve into a more sculptural Greek-revival style, which was then superseded by Italianate and rococo-revival designs. During the 1850s Longworth replaced the original mantelpieces with marble ones whose arched shape echoed the entryways he also added at the time. To embellish his renovated hallway Longworth engaged the artist Robert

Fig. 1 Entrance hall, Taft Museum.

Scott Duncanson to create the remarkable series of murals that is the most unusual element of the interior decoration of the house throughout its history.

Nicholas Longworth was a connoisseur and patron of European and American art. He actively supported both art institutions and individual artists and was particularly sympathetic to American painters and sculptors who, like himself, were born in the East and shared his vision of creating on the banks of the Ohio the Athens of the West.[10] Hiram Powers, Thomas Worthington Whittredge, and James Henry Beard were notable among that group. Also included was Duncanson, who was born in Fayette, New York, in 1821 and settled in Cincinnati, where he developed his style as a romantic landscape painter influenced by the Hudson River School. The murals Duncanson painted for Longworth, a series of eight large atmospheric landscape vignettes and five floral still lifes (the two American eagle overdoors being apparently of an earlier date), all in elaborately rendered trompe l'oeil gilt-wood rococo-revival frames, are rare examples of mid-nineteenth-century American wall painting (fig. 1). They conform to no specific precedent, although references both to English and French scenic wallpapers and to early-American mural painting are obvious.

Duncanson was an immature artist at the time of the Belmont commission. Since there is no indication he had undertaken such an ambitious project before, credit for the idea must be given to Longworth. In turn, it may be considered that these murals were but one part of a highly ambitious and integrated interior design scheme envisioned by the patron. That being the case, it is unknown to what extent such a scheme was completed since no contemporary mention of the murals has surfaced.[11]

By 1850, Cincinnati had grown tremendously and had become the largest furniture-making center in the country, exporting objects of every description in every direction along a network of rivers and lakes that provided easy and cheap transportation. This industry was based on a volume trade of simple, well-constructed furniture and efficiently supplied the continually expanding western markets. Although virtually everything was now locally produced, a few ambitious families sought out imported furniture for the highest quality objects. In *The Cincinnati Daily Gazette* of April 6, 1838, "a variety of household furniture part of which comes straight from Paris" was offered; and on August 4, 1841, there was a sale of "the furniture of a genteel private dwelling . . . almost nearly new and mostly of New York Manufacture."[12]

As his patronage of Duncanson and other artists attests, Longworth was a loyal enthusiast of local artists and artisans. As a collector of broad and confident taste, he was also in a position to furnish his home with acquisitions either imported into Cincinnati by an agent or purchased on his travels and shipped home directly by him. Without further documentation it can only be assumed that Longworth used all three methods to outfit Belmont as his showpiece for the romantic ideals of the mid-nineteenth-century American artistic community.

The first visual documents of the interior of the Baum-Taft House are photographs taken about 1925 during the residence of Anna Sinton and Charles Phelps Taft. David Sinton, Anna's father, had further enlarged the house after he acquired it in 1871. These early-twentieth-century photographs chart the evolution of taste of three generations of wealthy and sophisticated nineteenth-century American families. The bones of Martin Baum's late-federal interiors have remained, revealing classical proportions, refined woodwork, and delicate plaster ornament. Also retained are the further embellishments of Longworth's arched entryways and marble mantels, although at some point before Sinton purchased the house, the Duncanson murals were covered with wallpaper.

After David Sinton's death in 1900, Anna and Charles Taft began their collecting career in earnest. They rapidly accumulated a world-class art collection, which they impulsively expanded without necessarily considering how or where it would be displayed when it arrived at Pike Street. This art was purchased to be studied, enjoyed, and lived with. It was never the Tafts' intention that it play a role as decoration in a premeditated scheme or period re-creation. Yet these photographs of their home capture a distinctive, highly rarefied style of American interior. Opulent eclecticism was the vogue among wealthy Americans who had traveled widely and acquired aggressively during the last three decades of the nineteenth century. During the Tafts' residence disparate elements that might be labeled Renaissance, Turkish, Louis XV, aesthetic, and Empire were melded to create characteristically American gilded-age vignettes.

This taste for mixing styles was exemplified in the rooms and collections being created during the late nineteenth century by America's richest families, including the Morgans, Vanderbilts, and Havemeyers, and was showcased in 1883 and 1884 in a two-volume edition published by D. Appleton & Co., *Artistic Houses: The Most Beautiful and Celebrated Homes in the United States with Descriptions of the Art Treasures Contained Therein*. The significant difference between the Taft house and those featured in *Artistic Houses* was that (aside from the fact that, with only a handful of Chicago exceptions, they were all on the East Coast) the houses were newly constructed, and therefore the architecture was conceived with the same taste with which the objects were acquired. In contrast, by 1880 the Taft house was already of acknowledged historic significance. The Tafts certainly could have afforded, and at various times considered, building a new house or gallery for their collection but always decided against doing so. And thus, even as they conformed to the taste of their peers, their rooms retained the vestiges of early-American neoclassicism with the current style of interior decoration su-

Fig. 2 Long hall, Baum-Taft House, ca. 1925.

perficially applied. It is this sense of continuity that gives the house its individual, comfortable appearance.

The Reverend Charles Frederick Goss commented on this relaxed charm:

> The house neither in its architecture, furnishings, nor decoration makes any pretense to any particular style, nor is there any trace of that wretched thing so incompatible with the sense of home, the trail of a collector. Yet the architecture is predominately colonial and there is a notable and noted collection of pictures numbering some seventy-five canvases hanging properly here and there upon the walls in all the rooms. . . .
>
> There is a sense of great wealth spent lavishly but quietly for comfort and beauty. There is perfect harmony.[13]

A photograph from this period of the long hall illustrates perhaps not "perfect harmony" but rather the Tafts' highly personal eclecticism (fig. 2). Here, cases displaying their treasured collections of porcelains line walls covered with 1860s-style rococo-revival wallpaper in a pattern of large asymmetric C scrolls framing bouquets of roses that obscures the Duncanson murals underneath. The early woodwork, however, was left intact. Furniture of different periods is interspersed between the cases. On these heavily patterned walls are hung paintings and maiolica plates. Another painting sits on an elaborately carved easel, which rests casually against the wall. The plain wood floors are partially covered with oriental rugs, and lighting is provided by electric chandeliers and picture lights over the paintings.

The Green Room similarly shows the Tafts' eclectic tastes (fig. 3). Most curious to the contemporary eye is the arrangement of the paintings: Rembrandt's *Portrait of a Man Rising from His Chair* (see 1931.409, p. 153), for example, hangs in front of a drape and behind a sofa.

Fig. 3 Green Room, Baum-Taft House, ca. 1925.

It is placed curiously low and near the Van Dyck portrait (see 1931.447, p. 177), which over-whelms it. The walls of the room are hung with a medallion-in-diaper-patterned covering, and the parquet floors are bare. The furniture is upholstered in a highly figured tapestry or velvet fabric. In one corner of the room is the elaborately carved Renaissance-style cupboard Charles purchased in France in 1901 (see 1989.4, pp. 552–53), on which are placed three oriental porcelain vases. The small marquetry lyre-based table and the fireplace screen date from the late nineteenth century. In another view of this room the drapes are open to reveal lace under curtains. A single long Renaissance-revival cornice extends over the windows with a tall pier mirror between them. This treatment is typical of the 1860s.

The Flemish Library was the Tafts' most deliberate attempt at creating a cohesive "artistic" interior. Richard Cote has discussed the architectural features, including the elaborately carved mantelpiece. The walls of this room were hung with an embossed, imitation tooled-leather covering of the sort manufactured in Europe and fashionable in the United States during the 1880s and 1890s. The room was informally arranged with low tapestry-covered upholstered furniture gathered around a carved circular library table. The plain wood floors are bare. In the fireplace opening is a leaded-glass firescreen with a design of leaves and flowers asymmet-rically clustered in the Japanese style associated with such aesthetic artists as John La Farge and Louis Comfort Tiffany (fig. 4). The frame of the screen, however, is en suite with the mantel carving and is of a completely different character from the glass it supports.

Photographs of several views of the Music Room also exist. Some show it outfitted for summer with bare parquet floors and light floral-patterned upholstered pieces, while others show one large and several smaller oriental carpets scattered about the floor and striped satin slipcovers on all the seating furniture (fig. 5). The furniture is a varied mix of French and

Fig. 4 Fireplace and firescreen, Flemish library, Baum-Taft House, ca. 1925.

Fig. 5 North wall, Music Room, Baum-Taft House, ca. 1925.

English forms. Against one wall is a fashionable long banquette with six loose back cushions. In front of the banquette is a Regency-style Grecian bench and a glass display case, for small precious collectibles, sitting on a Louis XV–style base. On the opposite side of the room is the piano with a crystal candelabrum. Other candelabra sit on the mantel, and large multiarmed chandeliers provide the lighting. The two eighteenth-century French commodes by Pierre Roussel (see 1931.333–34, pp. 554–55) flank the arched entryway. Gilt ballroom chairs line the walls; groupings of oriental porcelains are arranged throughout; and, of course, pictures are everywhere.

On the walls behind the banquette and the piano a garland-swag applied plaster ornament and a gilt picture molding were added. Beneath these moldings velvet covered the walls to the baseboards, creating a background on which the paintings were hung in tiers. Between the bays of windows more pictures were double hung, and still others were placed on easels. Above the commodes hung the portraits of Charles and Anna Taft painted by Madrazo in 1904 (see 3.1931 and 4.1931, pp. 230 and 231).

Although lavish, the room was not formal. The furniture itself was comfortable and its arrangement casual, and the window treatments were light and simple. In character it suggests the English country-house drawing room more than a grand beaux-arts ballroom and conforms to the aesthetic advocated by Edith Wharton and Ogden Codman in their 1897 work *The Decoration of Houses,* which rejected the oppressive opulence of the preceding decades in favor of a more simple grandeur.[14]

By 1910, when the Tafts undertook to enlarge their dining room, this movement toward the purity of design advocated by the aristocratic Wharton and her young architect-cousin Codman had reformed the tastes of the American upper class. The Adamesque decoration

Fig. 6 Dining room, Baum-Taft House, ca. 1925.

that was chosen for the Tafts' dining room reflects this changed attitude (fig. 6). It is an interpretative, not literal, re-creation of a period design. Suitable to the scheme, the room was hung with the Tafts' collection of English portraits, including works by Gainsborough, Romney, and Reynolds, and furnished with reproduction Chippendale-style pieces. Thus, in the final major addition to the house, the completion of a full cycle in the changing tastes in nineteenth-century American interior design is demonstrated. Ironically, and perhaps inevitably, the Tafts turned for their inspiration to the same source as Baum had one hundred years earlier—namely, the refined neoclassicism of Robert Adam—yet created an unmistakably twentieth-century Georgian-revival environment.

Anna Taft's death in 1931 marked the beginning of the conversion of the Baum-Taft House to the Taft Museum. Walter Siple, then director of the Cincinnati Art Museum, was also named director of this new institution and undertook a major refurbishing of the building, both inside and out. Siple felt compelled to exhibit the Tafts' major and varied collections in a setting compatible with the architecture of the original house. To this end, he eliminated the vestiges of eclectic Victorian taste that Charles and Anna had chosen to live with. In the *Bulletin of the Cincinnati Art Museum* of January 1933, Siple explained his intentions regarding the tenor of the renovations: "Our idea with regard to the installation was to provide a dignified background for the Taft collections—this background to reflect the feelings of a home of the first quarter of the nineteenth century. . . . In order to do this, it was necessary to provide the rooms not only with window draperies, andirons and fenders, but also with floorcoverings and furniture."[15]

Obviously, his goal was not to establish a house museum in the sense that it is currently understood—namely, the display of the art and artifacts of a family, possibly spanning several generations, in the context in which they had been enjoyed. Rather, it was his vision to select a period in time, in this case the early nineteenth century, and to recreate idealized room settings based on the contemporary knowledge of that period. In this approach, Siple was conforming to the methodology of his colleagues in the developing field of American decorative arts study. Doubtless, Henry F. du Pont's 1930 remarks on his installations at Winterthur could have been Siple's as well when he explained, "I am doing the house architecturally and correctly, and I am paying greatest attention even to the epoch of the fringes."[16]

As an academic (he was a graduate of Paul Sachs's course in museology at Harvard and a former instructor at the Groton School in Connecticut), Walter Siple required a historic precedent on which to base his aesthetic choices. His surviving notes and letters include investigations into English, French, and American primary source materials and lengthy correspondence with the leading antiquarians and dealers in period textiles, wall coverings, and carpeting. When selecting paint colors for the various rooms, Siple decided to match the color of the oldest surviving layer of paint, wherever found. This method represented the current scholarship in the 1930s and was the one used at Colonial Williamsburg to determine the palette there. Modern scholars now rely on chemical analysis rather than visual matching of original samples. This analysis often reveals that paint undergoes dramatic changes in value and hue caused variously by the accumulation of dirt, fading, and fugitive pigments. Explaining his choices, Siple wrote: "In two of the rooms and the hall we found traces of the original tinting of the walls—powder blue, lemon yellow, and grey green. Here these colors have been used. Owing to the replastering of the other rooms it was not possible to determine what the wall treatment had been. In these we have used colors popular in the 1820s—grey, violet, and light blue."[17]

It should be noted here that despite Siple's commitment to returning the house to its first period, as an art scholar he recognized the significance of the Duncanson murals and oversaw their painstaking restoration.

After the wall colors were selected and the woodwork throughout the house was painted white, Siple decided to add wallpaper borders above the wainscoting in several of the rooms.[18] During Martin Baum's time such borders would have been used with less restraint than in Siple's installation. Then, wide borders were typically hung at cornice rather than chair-rail height, and narrower borders were often used at both levels, as well as vertically, to outline the architecture of the room. Also, they were often combined with a patterned paper rather than applied to plain painted walls. Siple obviously decided that bold-patterned walls would distract the twentieth-century eye from the art and therefore settled on this treatment that introduced neoclassical ornament and color to the rooms discreetly.

Siple carefully considered all window treatments. He researched the Regency drapery designs published in England by Rudolph Ackermann in *The Repository of the Arts and Sciences* during the 1820s, from which he noted such details as color schemes, cornices, sub-curtains, and rods. He also purchased original plates from Pierre de la Mésangère's magazine, *Meubles et objets de goût,* from Elinor Merrell, a New York dealer and expert in old chintzes and toiles de Jouy. It was from several of these de la Mésangère designs from the period that Siple adapted the curtains for the majority of the museum's rooms (fig. 7). The textiles used for these draperies were primarily nineteenth-century silks purchased from Elinor Merrell. Merrell also supplied the elaborate trims, which she had replicated in quantity when there was insufficient yardage of the original. The wooden rods and the tiebacks, which are carved and gilded in designs conforming to period prototypes, as well as the draperies, were fabricated in Cincinnati (fig. 8).

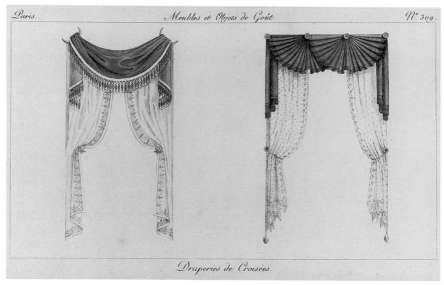

Fig. 7 Pierre de la Mésangère, *Meubles et objets de goût*
(Paris, 1805–19), "Draperies de Croisées," pl. no. 309.

In addition to the draperies styled from the de la Mésangère plates, Siple chose to make curtains for the President's Room and two of the smaller galleries from lengths of surviving early-nineteenth-century toiles de Jouy (fig. 9). Two designs, *Les Sphinx médaillons à l'antique* and *Le Lion amoureux* (see 1932.218 and 1932.217, pp. 117 and 116), were purchased from Merrell, and a third, *Le Romain* (see 1932.214, p. 118), from Edgar Ashley, another antique-textile dealer. Toiles de Jouy enjoyed a resurgence of popularity with both European and American decorators in the 1930s, and many of the original patterns were copied at that time. Although current museum practice would not condone the reworking and use of period textiles, curators of Siple's generation found this practice preferable to using reproductions for creating an "authentic" installation. Inevitably, these textiles have deteriorated since 1932. In 1989 the firm Brunschwig & Fils reproduced one of these patterns, *Les Sphinx,* and curtains made of this new fabric are now installed in the three galleries where the period toiles had hung (fig. 10).

Before moving to Cincinnati, Ella Siple, Walter Siple's wife, was the curator of decorative arts at the Worcester Art Museum in Massachusetts. She was a textile expert there, and at the Taft she was active in the educational programs. In many of Walter Siple's letters she is mentioned, and it must be acknowledged that she, too, contributed her expertise in these decisions.[19]

Siple investigated several possibilities for floor coverings and contacted a number of firms that manufactured reproduction Wilton and Axminster carpets and that dealt in antique rugs. He decided on reproduction strip carpeting from American mills to be sewn together into large area rugs rather than installed wall-to-wall, as was the practice during the 1820s (fig. 11). Siple explained his choice:

> The floorcoverings, reproductions or original carpets although not carried to the baseboards because of the difficulty of museum housekeeping, obviate the disagreeable clatter of bare floors in period rooms. We have also avoided the roping off of whole or parts of rooms as would have been necessary had we used valuable old carpets or rugs. It is our feeling that it was more important to preserve the home atmosphere, which results from free access to the rooms and comfortable seating facilities, than to give visitors mere glimpses into forbidden territory.[20]

Fig. 8 Lavender Room, Taft Museum, 1992.

Fig. 9 President's Room, Taft Museum, ca. 1932.

Fig. 10 President's Room, Taft Museum, 1992.

These carpets suffered the wear of thirty years and were replaced in the 1960s during Katherine Hanna's directorship with modern high-pile area rugs with classical-revival motifs.

Walter Siple selected the well-established New York firm of Edward F. Caldwell & Co. to manufacture the lighting fixtures for the museum. Caldwell had an excellent reputation for decorative metalwork and is highly regarded for the innovative designs it produced during the first decades of the twentieth century. For the Taft Museum, Siple requested electric-light fixtures based on early-nineteenth-century forms: for the entrance hall he wanted clear blown-glass lanterns with hanging chains and for the other corridors, both wall-mounted and hanging frosted-glass lanterns with smoke bells. Large chandeliers with antique brass finish and frosted cut-glass bowls and globes based on English Regency prototypes were made to specification and installed throughout the museum's rooms (see fig. 11). These lighting devices remain in the museum.

With the exception of the very few pieces considered part of the art collection, the furniture belonging to the Taft family was removed during the renovation. In his effort to create the mood of early-nineteenth-century interiors, in April 1932 Walter Siple purchased at auction at the Anderson Galleries in New York a significant group of American federal furniture. This furniture had belonged to the recently deceased collector and connoisseur Louis Guerineau Myers. Myers, who for much of his professional life served as the treasurer of the John D. Rockefeller Fund, had perceptively realized the artistic merit of areas of American decorative arts overlooked by the general audience.[21] Unlike many fellow collectors, Myers judged an

Fig. 11 Malta Gray Room, Taft Museum, ca. 1932.

object by aesthetic, rather than historical, criteria, thereby elevating utilitarian objects to fine-arts status. By 1921 he had auctioned his first collection, which consisted primarily of eighteenth-century furniture, much of it destined for institutions including Colonial Williamsburg and the Metropolitan Museum of Art.

Throughout the 1920s Myers continued to collect major pre-Revolutionary pieces, but he increasingly focused on the furniture of the early republic, especially that from the New York workshop of Duncan Phyfe. Myers contributed pieces from his collection to the Metropolitan Museum of Art's seminal exhibition of Phyfe furniture in 1922. In 1929 he and his wife, who was on the board of the National Council of Girl Scouts, organized the *Loan Exhibition of Eighteenth- and Early-Nineteenth-Century Furniture and Glass* from major private collections of American antiques to benefit that organization. This exhibition, which was held at the American Art Galleries in New York City, was an enormous success and is considered a landmark in the awakening of appreciation of these fields. In conjunction with the exhibition, Myers compiled a detailed illustrated catalogue in which he helped to define regional cabinet-making characteristics and which remains a valuable reference work. In it he wrote:

> Practically unknown a few years ago the name of Duncan Phyfe has today become the plaything of every auctioneer, every furniture dealer, and every furniture buyer in the country. Every man's work during the first half of the 19th century is foisted on poor Phyfe, and then he also has to shoulder many an Englishman's third rate product.
>
> The first thing we must recognize when trying to make attributions is that no cabinetmaker with any pretense of popularity can hope to do more than design and supervise the construction of his output. That means Phyfe no more worked with his own hands than did the famous

Chippendale. Then we also know that men trained in the shop of a master to certain proportions, methods and mechanics of construction often separate from him and continue to
reproduce the things his hand is accustomed to albeit more mechanically and less carefully.

And he continued:

Contemporaries of Phyfe not trained by him and reproducers of yesterday never succeed in
closely copying these various touches. Early nineteenth century cabinetmakers in Philadelphia,
Boston, and other large cities interpreted both the later Sheraton and classical styles, but not
one of them ever turned a leg or carved an acanthus leaf in the Phyfe manner. Whether their
methods were necessarily inferior to Phyfe's is, of course, a matter of personal predilection, but
competent judges incline to this belief.[22]

Thus, Siple's decision to outfit the Taft Museum with this furniture found corroboration in
its stylistic affinity with the architecture of the original Baum house and with current popular
taste. Neither his own research on the early furniture industry in Cincinnati nor the lack of
evidence of New York furniture being imported into Ohio during the early period diminished
his enthusiasm when he announced, "We were fortunate in obtaining several pieces of furniture from the workshop of Duncan Phyfe which were formerly in the Louis Guerineau Myers
collection."[23]

With the acquisition of these objects, the furniture at the Taft Museum transcended decoration and became part of the collection. Siple's purchases were mostly seating furniture—
four sofas and a number of side chairs—and small tables that enhanced the galleries rather
than created true domestic settings. He favored pieces with sculptural rather than architectural
qualities, avoiding forms such as secretaries, sideboards, or other casepieces that were available
in the collection. In all, twenty-nine lots from the sale—including mirrors, a clock, and other
small decorative objects—were chosen for their exemplary quality rather than for their rarity
of form. With only two exceptions, all the furniture was of New York manufacture and attributed by Myers to the workshop of Duncan Phyfe.

Since Myers's pioneering work in this area, much information on the furniture industry
in New York during the federal period has come to light. It is known that by 1805 over 125
artisans were engaged in allied furniture-making trades, and as with the rest of the city's in-
dustries that number was to grow vigorously in the next decades.[24] Pieces with the labels of
previously unidentified makers continue to surface, a significant number of whom would have
had contact with Phyfe's workshop in the fifty-five years it operated, from 1792 to 1847. Since
only three bills of sale and less than a dozen pieces labeled by Phyfe survive, only very little
of the large body of furniture produced in the style associated with him can be assigned to
his workshop.[25] Nor can quality be the sole criterion for attributions; although Phyfe is known
for creating the highest quality objects, his shop also produced mid-level goods, especially for
export. Similarly, other makers during the same period, including Charles-Honoré Lannuier
and Michael Allison, were crafting objects of the highest caliber. Although there are many
more pieces labeled by these two contemporaries of Phyfe than by Phyfe himself, they were
not recognized by Myers.

Since the refurbishment of the Taft Museum during the 1930s, additions and alterations
to the interiors have been restrained. In the dining room a reproduction sideboard and dining
table have been replaced with authentic examples, and a classical-revival card table has been
donated by Taft family members. The carpeting and textiles, as noted, continue to be replaced

as necessary. In concept, Walter Siple's vision for the display of the Taft collection has proven successful. After sixty years, the museum interiors have themselves become period settings that continue to offer insights into the evolution of the classical ideal in American design.

Notes

1. Marilyn Z. Ott, "Martin Baum," unpublished paper, Taft Museum In-School Program, Mar. 1975, with a bibliography added in 1977, p. 6. Ott does not identify the source of this 1864 quotation.

2. *Historical Places and Landmarks: Leading Manufacturers and Merchants of Cincinnati and Environs,* New York, 1886, p. 37.

3. Henry Howe, *Historical Collections of Ohio,* from a treatise of 1888 published by the State of Ohio in 1904, vol. I, p. 817, quoted in Jane Merkel, "The Baum-Taft House: A Historiography," *The Taft Museum: A Cincinnati Legacy,* Cincinnati, 1988, p. 36.

4. Merkel, p. 36.

5. Jane Sikes Hageman, *Ohio Furniture Makers, 1790 to 1845,* privately published, 1984, p. 11.

6. See Jane E. Sikes, *The Furniture Makers of Cincinnati, 1790 to 1849,* privately published, 1976, p. 192, for a copy of Benjamin Porter's bill to William Lytle, 1815.

7. Sikes, p. 14.

8. Sikes, p. 46.

9. *The Western Spy* [Cincinnati], Jan. 1820.

10. Abby S. Schwartz, "Nicholas Longworth: Art Patron of Cincinnati," *The Taft Museum: A Cincinnati Legacy,* Cincinnati, 1988, p. 18.

11. See Joseph D. Ketner II, "The Belmont Murals in the Taft Museum," *The Taft Museum: A Cincinnati Legacy,* Cincinnati, 1988, pp. 51–63, and also Ketner's catalogue entries (1932.233–235, 1931.23/–243) for a more complete description of these murals.

12. Sikes, p. 47.

13. Charles Frederick Goss, *Cincinnati, the Queen City: 1788–1912,* Chicago and Cincinnati, 1912, vol. I, p. 444.

14. Edith Wharton and Ogden Codman, Jr., *The Decoration of Houses,* New York, 1897.

15. Walter P. Siple, "The Taft Museum," *Bulletin of the Cincinnati Art Museum,* vol. IV, no. 1 (Jan. 1933), pp. 11–12.

16. Henry F. du Pont, in Elizabeth Stillinger, *The Antiquers,* New York, 1980, p. 224.

17. Siple, p. 7.

18. Some of these borders were original early-nineteenth-century examples purchased from the collection of Nancy McClelland, the leading authority on the use of wall coverings in early America.

19. This information was provided by Mrs. Charles King, former acting head of education at the Taft Museum.

20. Siple, p. 13.

21. Stillinger, p. 264.

22. Louis Guerineau Myers, *Loan Exhibition of Eighteenth- and Early-Nineteenth-Century Furniture and Glass for the Benefit of the National Council of Girl Scouts, Inc.,* exh. cat., American Art Galleries, New York, 1929, n.p.

23. Siple, p. 11.

24. Daniel Longworth, ed., *American Almanack, New York Register and City Directory for the Thirteenth Year of American Independence,* New York, 1805–6.

25. Jeanne Vibert Sloane, "A Duncan Phyfe Bill and the Furniture It Documents," *The Magazine Antiques,* vol. CXXXI, no. 5 (May 1987), p. 1107.

American Furniture

Lisa Krieger

Duncan Phyfe

Loch Fannich, Scotland 1768–1854 New York

Scottish-born Duncan Phyfe arrived in America in 1784 and settled in Albany, New York, with his widowed mother and siblings. By 1792 he had moved to New York City where his name appears as "Duncan Fife, joiner, at 2 Broad St." in William Duncan's *New York Directory and Register*. In 1794 he moved to 3 Broad Street and changed the spelling of his last name to Phyfe. He again relocated his business in 1795 to 35 Partition Street, which in the early nineteenth century became Fulton Street. He remained at that address until his retirement in 1847, expanding his enterprise into what became the largest and most fashionable cabinet shop in New York.

Phyfe's early work was strongly influenced by the English Sheraton style. He became identified with the use of high-quality woods, most often Cuban or Santo Domingan mahogany, and restrained ornamental treatments. His furniture skillfully combined turning, reeding, and contrasting veneer work with carved embellishment. Neoclassical motifs, especially acanthus leaves, cornucopias, drapery swags, lyres, thunderbolts, and rosettes were his favored decorations. After 1815 Phyfe's work shows an increasing awareness of contemporary French design in the Directoire and Consulate styles.

During Phyfe's fifty-five-year career, his output was prolific, and he employed over one hundred tradesmen. However, fewer than fifteen pieces of furniture bearing his shop's label have been identified, and only three documented bills of sale are known.

After Phyfe's retirement in 1847 he auctioned his inventory and remained at his house at 169 Fulton Street until his death.

1932.34

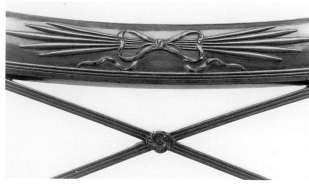

1932.34

Possibly Duncan Phyfe

Pair of Side Chairs

New York, 1805–15
Mahogany, h. 84.3 x w. (seat) 48.3 x D. 42.5 cm (33⅛ x 19 x 16¾ in.)

Many of the features found on this pair of side chairs closely resemble features on the set of twelve chairs that Duncan Phyfe made in 1807 for William Bayard (fig. 1).[1] The similarities include bell-shaped seats, swept-back Grecian rear legs, reeded, double-cross banister backs with carved rosettes at the centers, and scroll-back top rails with tablets carved with a cluster of five reeds bound with a bowknot. The curved stiles are reeded on their faces and finished on their outer sides with an applied, turned bos. These stiles, which widen at the point where the reeding stops, gently curve into tapering square rear legs. The front legs of the Taft chairs are turned and reeded in an adaptation of the Sheraton style favored in New York, while the Bayard chairs have square, tapered saber legs, a more unusual and stylized treatment.

Fig. 1 Duncan Phyfe, *Side Chair*, New York, 1807. Mahogany, H. 83.8 x w. 48.3 x D. 55.4 cm (33 x 19 x 21⅛ in.). Winterthur, Del., courtesy The Henry du Pont Winterthur Museum.

Several other examples closely related to the Taft chairs include one, attributed to Duncan Phyfe, in the collection of the New York State Museum in Albany,[2] and a version with arms, which, like the Taft chairs, also once belonged to Louis Guerineau Myers and displays slight variations in the carved-reed-and-bowknot motif, now in the Metropolitan Museum of Art.[3]

Scroll-back chairs based on ancient Greek and Roman prototypes first appeared in *The London Chairmaker's and Carver's Book of Prices for Workmanship* in 1802. These designs were quickly translated into an American idiom. Interpreted by craftsmen such as Duncan Phyfe, the form developed its distinctive and arguably highest expression in New York. As Charles Montgomery has explained, Phyfe was in an excellent position to assume leadership in the dissemination of this new classical style, which shortly after his death became synonymous with his name.[4] Yet, despite the fact that Phyfe remained a dominant figure in the New York furniture industry for nearly half a century, remarkably few pieces can substantively be documented to him—and fewer still of this particular early style.[5]

1. Charles F. Montgomery, *American Furniture of the Federal Period*, New York, 1966, p. 120.

2. John L. Scherer, *New York Furniture of the Federal Period, 1788–1825*, Albany, N.Y., 1988, p. 26.

3. New York, The Metropolitan Museum of Art, inv. no. 31.44.2; also see a pair sold at Sotheby's, New York, Jan. 29, 1983, no. 398, and one chair

sold at Christie's, New York, Oct. 18, 1986, no. 492, with an exposed seat rail.

4. Montgomery, p. 117.

5. Only the label of Duncan Phyfe designates firmly attributed pieces; others have been identified as being from his shop through bills of sale and family records.

Provenance Louis Guerineau Myers, New York (sale, American Art Association, Anderson Galleries, Inc., New York, Apr. 7–9, 1932, no. 536); Taft Museum purchase, Apr. 9, 1932.

Literature Nancy McClelland, *Duncan Phyfe and the English Regency, 1795–1850*, New York, 1939, p. 174, pl. 156.

1932.33, 1932.34

Possibly Duncan Phyfe

Side Chair

New York, 1805–15
Mahogany, H. 84 x w. (seat) 48 x D. 43.9 cm (33⅜ x 18⅞ x 17¼ in.)

This side chair displays several of the variations on the popular scroll-back style offered by New York chairmakers during the

1932.14

early nineteenth century. In contrast to the design of the preceding pair (see 1932.33–34), this example features a reeded, exposed seat rail and slightly shorter legs, which result in a weightier appearance. Also different are the vase turnings at the bottom of the stiles just below the stay rail. This more costly option breaks the continuous line of the rear profile and contributes to the more substantial character of this chair.

The popular motif of a cluster of reeds bound with a bowknot again appears carved on the tablet of the crest rail of this chair.[1]

1. See Charles Over Cornelius, *Furniture Masterpieces of Duncan Phyfe,* Garden City, N.Y., 1928, pl. 11, and Nancy McClelland, *Duncan Phyfe and the English Regency, 1795–1850,* New York, 1939, p. 175, pl. 157, for similar examples.

Provenance Louis Guerineau Myers, New York (sale, American Art Association, Anderson Galleries, Inc., New York, Apr. 7–9, 1932, no. 482); Taft Museum purchase, Apr. 9, 1932.

Exhibition New York, American Art Galleries, *Loan Exhibition of Eighteenth- and Early-Nineteenth-Century Furniture and Glass for the Benefit of the National Council of Girl Scouts, Inc.,* Sept. 25–Oct. 9, 1929 (cat. by Louis Guerineau Myers, no. 787).

1932.14

§▲

Possibly Duncan Phyfe

Side Chair

New York, 1805–15
Mahogany, H. 83.8 x w. (seat) 48.3 x D. 43 cm (33 x 19 x 16⅞ in.)

Similar to the preceding example (see 1932.14), this scrolled, double-cross-back side chair features more elaborate and costly carved embellishments. The tablet in the crest rail displays finely rendered sheaves of wheat bound with a bowknot, and the vase turnings on the stiles are further ornamented with vertical waterleafs on their lower sections. A chair virtually twin to the Taft example in the Metropolitan Museum of Art is attributed to Duncan Phyfe's workshop (inv. no. 1976.197).

The upper right cross brace of this chair had been restored at the time of purchase.

Provenance Louis Guerineau Myers, New York (sale, American Art Association, Anderson Galleries, Inc., New York, Apr. 7–9, 1932, no. 537); Taft Museum purchase, Apr. 9, 1932.

Literature Nancy McClelland, *Duncan Phyfe and the English Regency, 1795–1850,* New York, 1939, p. 174, pl. 156.

1932.35

1932.35

§▲
Side Chairs

New York, ca. 1815
Mahogany with satinwood veneers, H. 82.6 x w. 44.8 x D. 47 cm (32½ x 17⅝ x 18½ in.)

The eight cane-seated side chairs that make up this set illustrate several heightened refinements of the scroll-back form that evolved in New York during the first decades of the nineteenth century. The convex curve of the rear stiles, which continues uninterrupted to concave-curved rear legs, creates a graceful profile derived from the antique *klismos* chair. A complex balance of line is further developed by the construction of the side rails, which are tenoned into the rear stiles and create the illusion of a second unbroken curve, this one extending from the crest rail to the front seat rail. The two front legs, again concave curves, are tenoned into the side rails and the front seat rail. The reeding that extends the entire length of the front face as well as across the front seat rail accentuates the linear flow of the design and relieves the flatness of the surface. Turned mahogany bosses are applied at the juncture of the front and side seat rails.

The crest rail is gently rolled and curved, and a panel, defined by a beaded edge, is veneered with figured mahogany. The splat,

1932.17—24

1932.17—24

1932.17—24

ornamented with both carved and contrasting wood, is the focus of the design. It consists of two horizontal pairs of clustered, stylized carved mahogany feathers supporting an oval medallion edged in mahogany with a satinwood veneer center. The design for this splat is illustrated in outline in plate number 6 of the *New York Book of Prices for Manufacturing Cabinet and Chair Work* for 1817 and is described as having "double Prince of Wales feathers, tied with a Gothic moulding."[1]

Classical references in chair design inspired by recent archaeological finds—such as the scrolled back and the saber leg, the latter feature known as the Greek leg—began to appear on New York furniture during the first years of the nineteenth century, almost immediately after their publication by such English de-

signers as Thomas Sheraton, Thomas Hope, and George Smith. The first documented example of the curved Greek leg in New York appears on the set, now in the Winterthur collection, that Duncan Phyfe billed to William Bayard on November 21, 1807. Also at Winterthur is a sketch attributed to Phyfe showing a lyre-splat side chair with scrolled back and saber legs of the same form as the Taft chairs. Charles Montgomery has dated that sketch to 1815–16 (fig. 1).[2]

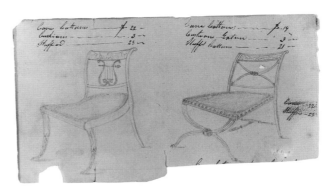

Fig. 1 Attributed to Duncan Phyfe, *Sketch for Lyre-splat Side Chair with Scrolled Back and Saber Legs.* Winterthur, Del., courtesy The Winterthur Library, Joseph Downs Collection of Manuscripts and Printed Ephemera, no. 56 x 6.4.

These two documents establish Phyfe as the preeminent proponent in the United States of this chair style, which in turn was firmly based on English Regency prototypes. Yet his designs are neither mere copies nor simplifications. Rather, they are refinements of the English examples, purer of form and more restrained in ornament, managing to appear at once delicate and substantial.

The highest quality materials and construction are evident on this set of chairs, but no documentation has surfaced to associate them with Phyfe, or any other chairmaker. There is, however, a set of eight cane-seat, scroll-back side chairs, documented as made by Phyfe in 1816, that in many respects appears closely related to the Taft set. The Phyfe chairs, made for James Brinkerhoff, have lyre splats and carved paw feet on the front legs—two common options offered on this style.[3]

Several other examples of chairs with splats of a similar design are known. McClelland illustrates three of these variants: one with arms, one with acanthus-carved front legs,[4] and another with hairy paw feet.[5] All of these have slip rather than caned seats, as does the pair in the Metropolitan Museum of Art, which is similar to the Taft chairs but lacks the satinwood veneer in the splat medallions (inv. nos. 26.104.2−3). Another variation of this form and one often seen on English examples is the spiral and twisted crest rail.[6] Painted fancy chairs were also made in this design.[7]

1. Charles F. Montgomery, *American Furniture of the Federal Period*, New York, 1966, p. 104.

2. Montgomery, p. 126.

3. Jean Vibert Sloane, "A Duncan Phyfe Bill and the Furniture It Documents," *The Magazine Antiques*, vol. CXXXI, no. 5 (May 1987), p. 1112, fig. 7.

4. Nancy McClelland, *Duncan Phyfe and the English Regency, 1795−1850*, New York, 1939, p. 178, pl. 161.

5. McClelland, p. 179, pl. 162. See also Patricia E. Kane, *Three Hundred Years of American Seating Furniture from the Collection of Mabel Brady Garvan and Other Collections at Yale University*, Boston, 1976, p. 176, pl. 156.

6. Louis Guerineau Myers, *Loan Exhibition of Eighteenth- and Early-Nineteenth-Century Furniture and Glass for the Benefit of the National Council of Girl Scouts, Inc.*, exh. cat., American Art Galleries, New York, 1929, no. 771. See also the Metropolitan Museum of Art, inv. no. 40.44.2.

7. Savery sale, Christie's, New York, June 1979, no. 271.

Provenance Louis Guerineau Myers, New York (sale, American Art Association, Anderson Galleries, Inc., New York, Apr. 7−9, 1932, no. 497, ill.); Taft Museum purchase, Apr. 9, 1932.

1932.17−24

Easy Chair

New York?, 1800−1810
Mahogany, yellow pine, and white pine; H. 101.6 x W. (seat) 69.9 x D. 68.6 cm (40 x 27½ x 27 in.)

Sharp perpendicular geometry dominates the design of this upholstered chair. The pine frame has a straight, sharply canted

1932.30

rectangular back, a straight front rail, and straight sides that are tempered only by a slight roll at their tops. The mahogany legs are ring-turned and tapered and sit atop brass cuffs and casters. The rear legs are square and raked. The chair has been reupholstered with modern spring-seat construction. It has a button-tufted back and a separate loose seat cushion and is covered with a woven, patterned red haircloth.

The precise rectilinear form of this chair is in direct juxtaposition with the design of most American examples preceding it. The majority of early-federal easy chairs were based on Queen Anne and Chippendale styles that had been only slightly modified over the course of more than fifty years. Those designs depended on an elaborate series of curves and usually incorporated saddle-shaped wings, scrolled arms, and arched crests. In concept, the Taft chair relates not to American prototypes but instead to eighteenth-century French design, specifically to the type of bergère, or closed-arm, chair introduced during the reign of Louis XVI. That chair style, which remained popular in France during the Restoration period of the early nineteenth century, likewise had a straight rectangular back and straight sides and legs. Unlike the French chair type, however, the Taft chair has no show wood on its frame, resulting in its severe, almost abstract appearance.

The previous owner of this chair, Louis Guerineau Myers, gave Philadelphia as the chair's place of origin without further explanation. Its design, however, is similar to another chair owned by Myers, also with reeded front legs and an old New

1932.30

York provenance, that he attributed to Duncan Phyfe.[1] The present chair fits both stylistically and in terms of construction with the types generally associated with New York.

1. The Phyfe chair is illustrated in Nancy McClelland, *Duncan Phyfe and the English Regency, 1795–1850*, New York, 1939, pl. 94, and is also illustrated in Louis Guerineau Myers, *Loan Exhibition of Eighteenth- and Early-Nineteenth-Century Furniture and Glass for the Benefit of the National Council of Girl Scouts, Inc.*, exh. cat., American Art Galleries, New York, 1929, no. 757.

Provenance Louis Guerineau Myers, New York (sale, American Art Association, Anderson Galleries, Inc., New York, Apr. 7–9, 1932, no. 528); Taft Museum purchase, Apr. 9, 1932.

1932.30

🌿

Attributed to the workshop of Duncan Phyfe

Scroll-back Sofa

New York, 1805–15
Mahogany, with secondary wood of maple; H. 95.3 x W. 198.1 x D. 76.2 cm (37½ x 78 x 30 in.)

Sofas of this type, with scrolled tripartite tablet crest rails, from which extend scrolled arms supported by turned arm supports, were extremely popular in New York during the first two decades of the nineteenth century. The Taft sofa is a fine and well-documented example of this form and was noted by Louis Guerineau Myers as being "slightly heavier than the others, the cresting rail particularly being wider."[1] On this example, the

1932.36

1932.36

crest rail, divided into three panels by a beaded edge, has a carved drapery swag tied with tassels and a bowknot at its center, flanked by clusters of five reeds tied with bowknots. This sequence of motifs frequently appears on sofas of this and related forms.[2]

The reeded arms of this sofa scroll straight down rather than curve inward, a common variation of the form, and are supported by turned members consisting of a ball-topped, tapered, and reeded shaft surmounting an inverted leaf-carved baluster. The four front legs are turned, reeded shafts atop urn-shaped cuffs that in turn sit on brass casters. The four rear legs are squared, tapered, and canted outward. The bell-shaped seat is upholstered over its front rail and has a tufted loose cushion. It is covered with charcoal-and-black-striped haircloth. When purchased in 1932 by the Taft Museum from the Louis Guerineau Myers collection, this sofa had only three rear legs and was covered with blue brocade (fig. 1).[3]

The Taft sofa has been identified by McClelland as one of a group of four "identical" sofas made by Duncan Phyfe. She illustrates a sofa apparently twin to the Taft's with matching striped haircloth covering, which—according to family history—Phyfe made for John Alling of Newark, New Jersey. McClelland also illustrates Jeremiah Pierson's sofa, which has rosettes carved on the front corner blocks, and mentions a fourth of the group as having been made for Theodore Frelinghuysen.[4]

Based on McClelland's research, one can assume that the Taft sofa came from the workshop of Duncan Phyfe. However, judging from the large number of surviving variations of this form, it must also be acknowledged that other unidentified New York workshops were manufacturing sofas of this configuration until after 1815, when the form was superseded by more literally neoclassical Grecian forms.

1. Noted in *The Private Collection of the Late Louis Guerineau Myers,* sale cat., American Art Association, New York, 1932, no. 540.

2. See New York, The Metropolitan Museum of Art, inv. no. 31.44.66, and Sotheby's, New York, Jan. 29, 1983, collection of Mr. Charles O. Smith, lot 390.

3. After its acquisition, it was restored to its present appearance with four rear legs and haircloth covering, although no records exist in the Taft Museum archives to document the restoration.

1932.36

Fig. 1 Attributed to the workshop of Duncan Phyfe, *Scroll-back Sofa with Blue Brocade,* in *The Private Collection of the Late Louis Guerineau Myers,* sale cat., no. 540, p. 157. New York, American Art Association, 1932.

1932.10

4. Nancy McClelland, *Duncan Phyfe and the English Regency, 1795–1850,* New York, 1939, pls. 237 (the Alling sofa, with upholstery identical to that of the Taft sofa), 281 (the Pierson sofa), p. 250 (the Frelinghuysen sofa).

Provenance Louis Guerineau Myers, New York (sale, American Art Association, Anderson Galleries, Inc., New York, Apr. 7–9, 1932, no. 540 [ill.]); Taft Museum purchase, Apr. 9, 1932.

Literature Nancy McClelland, *Duncan Phyfe and the English Regency, 1795–1850,* New York, 1939, p. 252.

1932.36

℘

Classical Sofa

New York, 1815–25
Mahogany and mahogany veneers, with secondary woods of maple and tulip poplar; H. 83.8 x W. 233.7 x D. 66 cm (33 x 92 x 26 in.)

By 1815 in New York, sofas with outward curving S-scrolled arms and winged paw feet replaced the straight-sided, turned-leg Sheraton styles as the most fashionable. This design, often referred to as a Grecian sofa, was derived from the reclining couches of the ancient Greeks and Romans and was so popular that it was adapted for contemporary use in numerous variations, including single-armed and armless *rcamiers,* and condensed into backless window seats and benches.

This sofa is a typical example of mid-period New York classical-revival furniture. It is solidly constructed of high-quality

mahogany with a tripartite crest rail enhanced by choice mahogany veneers—crotch in the center and fiddleback in the two side panels. The scrolled, reeded frame is supported on four well-carved lion's-paw feet, the front ones bracketed with eagle wings and oak-leaf-scrolled volutes. Upholstered with a loose cushion in black haircloth with brass tacking, it rests on brass casters.

The several examples of comparable surviving sofas have traditionally been attributed to Duncan Phyfe, generally based on a comparison with the one published by Charles Over Cornelius

1932.10

in his early work, *Furniture Masterpieces of Duncan Phyfe*.[1] However, numerous variations in the designs of both the crest rails and the wings and paws are evident on all these examples, pointing to the fact that New York workshops other than Phyfe's were producing this design. In fact, only one example can be assuredly identified as from the shop of Duncan Phyfe—the caned, lyre-armed sofa made for James Lefferts Brinkerhoff in 1816, which survives with its accompanying bill of sale in a private collection.[2]

A sofa now in the New York State Museum in Albany displays some of the variations on this form.[3] Like the Taft's, it has a veneered tripartite crest rail, but the veneers are less figured and highly contrasting. Its winged leg brackets have many more feathers and two smaller scrolled volutes, rather than one large one. These subtle distinctions, inherent in the handmade nature of furniture of this period, make attribution to any one maker or workshop extremely tentative without additional history or documentation.

1. Charles Over Cornelius, *Furniture Masterpieces of Duncan Phyfe*, Garden City, N.Y., 1928, pl. xvi.

2. Jean Vibert Sloane, "A Duncan Phyfe Bill and the Furniture It Documents," *The Magazine Antiques*, vol. cxxxi, no. 5 (May 1987), p. 1107, pl. ii. On Oct. 10, 1987, Christie's, New York (no. 219), sold a sofa, and in Jan. 1988, Hirshl and Adler Galleries, New York, sold another—both of similar form and both attributed to Phyfe.

3. John L. Scherer, *New York Furniture of the Federal Period, 1788–1825*, Albany, N.Y., 1988, p. 24. This sofa was sold at Christie's, New York, June 24, 1980, no. 704.

Provenance Louis Guerineau Myers, New York (sale, American Art Association, Anderson Galleries, Inc., New York, Apr. 7–9, 1932, no. 338); Taft Museum purchase, Apr. 8, 1932.

1932.10

Michael Allison

1773–1855

American-born Michael Allison, whose career spanned nearly half a century, was a cabinetmaker in New York City. His early work in the federal style was influenced by Hepplewhite designs, while his later output of classical-revival furniture was similar to that of his contemporary and competitor Duncan Phyfe. A number of pieces bearing various labels from Allison's Vesey Street shops survive, including one from 1817 reading *M. Allison's Cabinet & Upholstery Furniture Warehouse No. 46 & 48 Vesey St., N.Y., N.Y.*

❧

Possibly by Michael Allison

Classical Sofa

New York, 1815–25
Mahogany and mahogany veneers, with secondary woods of maple and mahogany; H. 86.4 x W. 233.7 x D. 66 cm
(34 x 92 x 26 in.)

Similar in form to the preceding sofa (see 1932.10), this example also has a gently rolled back with a tripartite crest rail of veneered, well-figured mahogany and a reeded frame with swan-neck-curved arms ending in turned paterae (small flat circular or oval ornaments)—all characteristics of its type. Less typical, however, are the rectangular reserves, which are relief-carved with bowed and tasseled drapery swags on a stippled ground, found on the frame above the front feet. The sofa is supported

1932.161

1932.161

by four carved lion's-paw feet, the two front ones emanating from foliate volutes and eagle wings. They rest on brass casters.

Numerous examples of this wing-and-paw-foot design exist, and individual characteristics indicating different carvers or workshops appear within the type. The legs of this sofa are muscular and massive, the ankles being thicker and the feet squarer than are frequently seen. Four separate wing feathers overlap yet remain distinct. Atop the foot are three leaves and a small tight volute on a punch-stippled ground.

Louis Guerineau Myers attributed this sofa to Duncan Phyfe and describes the feet "as worthy of admiration as the paw feet of Phyfe's superlative lyre-back chairs."[1] However, when compared with the documented wing-and-paw feet of the sofa made by Phyfe for James Lefferts Brinkerhoff,[2] they bear little more than the most general of similarities. The feathers of the Phyfe sofa are tightly furled, the volutes are smaller, and in general the design is sleeker and more stylized.

By contrast, the legs of this sofa relate more closely to those on a card table attributed to Michael Allison in the collection of the New York State Museum in Albany.[3] On that robust and imaginative table, winged supports that evolve into eagle's-head feet are designed and carved in a manner similar enough to the brackets on the Taft sofa to suggest that both pieces are the product of the same hand.

Michael Allison was one of Phyfe's primary competitors in New York, and his career was nearly as long.[4] A number of labeled Allison pieces have survived, and whereas his early output favored inlaid work in the Hepplewhite style, his later work consistently reveals a taste for energetic, heavily carved ornament.

The drapery swag in rectangular reserve appears on several pieces of documented Allison furniture, as on the aprons of a pair of card tables made for Lucinda Newcomb[5] and on another five-legged card table made for Frederick Shonnard.[6] While by no means exclusive to Allison,[7] this motif was evidently a favorite of his, and its appearance on the Taft sofa, in conjunction with the character of the winged feet, indicates that it could possibly have originated in his shop.

1. *The Private Collection of the Late Louis Guerineau Myers,* sale cat., American Art Association, New York, 1932, no. 337.

2. Jean Vibert Sloane, "A Duncan Phyfe Bill and the Furniture It Documents," *The Magazine Antiques,* vol. CXXXI, no. 5 (May 1987), p. 1106.

3. John L. Scherer, *New York Furniture of the Federal Period, 1788–1825,* Albany, N.Y., 1988, p. 26; see cover detail.

4. Gregor Norman-Wilcox, "Michael Allison and a Sideboard," *Connoisseur* (July 1969), pp. 203–7. Phyfe worked 1792–1847; Allison, 1796–1847.

5. Nancy McClelland, *Duncan Phyfe and the English Regency, 1795–1850,* New York, 1939, pl. 187. Also see Elizabeth Stillinger, *The Antiques Guide to Decorative Arts in America, 1600–1875,* New York, 1972, p. 298.

6. *The Magazine Antiques* (Sept. 1946), p. 176.

7. A table virtually identical to the Shonnard one in the Museum of the City of New York and illustrated in *Furniture by New York Cabinetmakers,* exh. cat., Museum of the City of New York, New York, 1956, is attributed to Phyfe; and a table with this motif that belonged to James Brinkerhoff is attributed to Charles-Honoré Lannuier. See Sloane, p. 1113.

Provenance Louis Guerineau Myers, New York (sale, American Art Association, Anderson Galleries, Inc., New York, Apr. 7–9, 1932, no. 337 [ill.]); Taft Museum purchase, Apr. 8, 1932.

1932.161

Classical Sofa

New York, 1815–25
Mahogany, H. 83.5 x W. 243.2 x D. 68.3 cm (32⅞ x 95¾ x 26⅞ in.)

Of the three classical sofas in the Taft Museum collection, this one is the most ornamented. Like the others, it has swan-neck-scrolled and reeded arms and a gently rolled back. Its crest rail, however, is carved with an unusual interpretation of the cornucopia motif. Although cornucopias appear frequently on New York federal furniture,[1] this adaptation is different in several ways. First, the two horns turn downward at the center of the rail where they cross and meet, rather than upward as is typically seen. Second, sheaves of wheat spill from the horns and extend the entire length of the crest rail. On other examples, a few stalks are combined with fruit and contained within a single panel. In his description of this detail, Louis Guerineau Myers wrote that no other example of this treatment had been seen,[2] but in 1939 McClelland illustrated the Taft sofa and described another "identical" sofa owned by Charles H. Sherrill.[3]

The second distinctive, if less rare, feature of this sofa is its legs and feet. When compared with the two other wing-and-paw-foot sofas at the Taft (see 1932.10, p. 95, and 1932.161, p. 96),

1932.26

1932.26

1932.26

these legs and feet appear to be coarsely carved. This trait, how-ever, can be explained by the fact that they were carved of a soft wood and that originally the wings and volutes were gilded and the feet painted verdigris, a popular treatment for New York classical furniture. Before the sofa was acquired by the museum, the painted surfaces were removed, a fact noted by Myers and quoted in his sale catalogue. With their original surface intact, the legs and feet of this sofa would, in fact, resemble those on the lyre-armed sofa made by Duncan Phyfe for James Brinkerhoff more closely than those on either of the other two examples.[4]

1. See Berry Tracy, *Federal Furniture and Decorative Arts at Boscobel*, New York, 1981, figs. 10 and 10a, for use of this motif by Phyfe.

2. Louis Guerineau Myers, *Loan Exhibition of Eighteenth- and Early-Nineteenth-Century Furniture and Glass for the Benefit of the National Council of Girl Scouts, Inc.*, exh. cat., American Art Galleries, New York, 1929, no. 505.

3. Nancy McClelland, *Duncan Phyfe and the English Regency, 1795–1850*, New York, 1939, p. 168, pl. 150.

4. Jean Vibert Sloane, "A Duncan Phyfe Bill and the Furniture It

Documents," *The Magazine Antiques,* vol. CXXXI, no. 5 (May 1987), p. 1106.

Provenance Louis Guerineau Myers, New York (sale, American Art Association, Anderson Galleries, Inc., New York, Apr. 7–9, 1932, no. 505 [ill.]); Taft Museum purchase, Apr. 9, 1932.

Literature *Fine Arts* (Apr. 1932), ill., p. 9 (adv.); Nancy McClelland, *Duncan Phyfe and the English Regency, 1795–1850,* New York, 1939, p. 168, pl. 150.

1932.26

⸎
Table Desk

New York, ca. 1810
Mahogany and mahogany veneers, H. 86.1 x W. 47 x D. 35.2 cm (33⅞ x 18½ x 13⅞ in.)

This desk is constructed with a plain mahogany oblong, hinged top that opens to reveal a green-baize-covered writing board, which, in turn, can be adjusted to various writing angles by means of another hinge. Beneath the writing board is a storage well, and beside it is a compartment fitted to accommodate ink bottles. The case below is built with one false and one function-ing drawer, both with cock-beaded edges and stamped brass pulls and key escutcheons. The front stiles of the case are reeded on line with the drawer fronts. Supporting the case, four turned and reeded legs with ring capitals and cuffs sit atop blocks, where they join a shaped mahogany shelf. Beneath these blocks are characteristic New York ring-and-vase feet with brass ball fer-rules.

1932.28

1932.28

When compared with other table desks, including the two formerly owned by Berry Tracy,[1] this one is more diminutive in scale and attenuated in proportion than is typical. It also lacks a sliding side drawer or candle shelf often found on this form and was most likely custom-ordered for a specific room.

Small, dual-purpose desks such as this one (desks that also served as small tables), often referred to as ladies' writing tables, were a popular if not altogether practical item with New Yorkers during the first three decades of the nineteenth century. The Taft desk, with its simple decoration, elegant proportions, and fine workmanship, is an early model, probably made about 1810. It is an example of the cabinetmaking industry's response to the many new forms of portable luxury furniture to be used in lit-erary and artistic pursuits that were introduced through the English design books of the late eighteenth and very early nine-teenth centuries.

1. Sale, Sotheby's, New York, *Important American Furniture: The Collection of the Late Berry B. Tracy,* Feb. 1, 1985, nos. 734, 768.

Provenance Louis Guerineau Myers, New York (sale, American Art Association, Anderson Galleries, Inc., New York, Apr. 7–9, 1932, no. 522 [ill.]); Taft Museum purchase, Apr. 9, 1932.

1932.28

1932.1

1932.1

Card Table

Boston-Salem area, ca. 1800
Mahogany with rosewood and satinwood veneers,
H. 74.9 x W. 94.6 x D. (closed) 46.4 cm (29½ x 37¼ x 18¼ in.)

When the Taft Museum furniture collection was assembled in 1932, this Massachusetts card table was one of only two pieces not of New York origin purchased from the Louis Guerineau Myers collection. It is an outstanding example of the fluid, serpentine form closely adapted from those published by Sheraton and Hepplewhite and favored by coastal, northern New England craftsmen from the 1790s until well into the 1820s. This shape, described in price books of the period as a square with serpentine front and ends and ovolo corners over colonnettes,[1] was inherently challenging to construct because of the complexity of the curves. Often, as on this example, the sculptural qualities of these tables were accentuated through the use of contrasting inlaid veneers and stringing on the edges of the leaves and on the skirts and colonnettes. The inlaid oval outlined in satinwood and framed in cross-cut rosewood is another detail typical of this type.

Far less characteristic, however, are the foliate, carved capitals atop the legs of the Taft table. It is this additional embellishment that elevates it above the numerous other well-proportioned and finely detailed tables, such as the one attributed to William Hook of Salem in the Museum of Fine Arts, Boston, which has the far more common ring-and-drum-turned capitals.[2] The turnings of the feet of the Taft table, with their ring and bulb above a high cuff and tapered ends, are also more complicated than is generally seen.

When this table is compared with the following Philadelphia card table, the different regional interpretations of the same fundamental form are clearly evident. The most obvious distinction is the New England predisposition to delicate, attenuated design in contrast to Philadelphia's preference for more substantial proportions.

1. Benjamin A. Hewitt, Patricia E. Kane, and Gerald W. R. Ward, *The Work of Many Hands: Card Tables in America, 1790–1820*, exh. cat., Yale University Art Gallery, New Haven, 1982, p. 86.
2. Hewitt et al., p. 134.

Provenance Louis Guerineau Myers, New York (sale, American Art Association, Anderson Galleries, Inc., New York, Apr. 7–9, 1932, no. 94); Taft Museum purchase, Apr. 7, 1932.

1932.1

Card Table

Philadelphia, ca. 1810
Mahogany and mahogany veneers, with secondary woods of red pine and eastern white pine; H. 74.9 x W. 90.8 x D. 44.5 cm (29½ x 35¾ x 17½ in.)

This card table is a refined and typically Philadelphia interpretation of Thomas Sheraton's designs and is derived from examples such as plate 9 of his book *The Cabinetmaker's and Upholsterer's Drawing Book,* published in London in 1802. Its top is an unusual variation on the simple rectangle, having a hinged leaf with straight sides, square ends, and serpentine front.[1] The edges of the leaves are deeply reeded. On the apron is a centered, raised tablet that relieves the plainness of the front and balances the area between the distinctive detail of raised and reeded panels on the pilasters. The three fixed legs and the fourth fly leg all have two narrow double rings above a capital ornamented only on the front with carved acanthus foliage. The shafts of the legs are tapered and reeded and terminate in a ring-banded and bulbous turning above a high rounded base.

1932.2

1932.2

The playing surface inside the top leaf is covered with green ivy-patterned felt dating from the second half of the nineteenth century.

When this table was auctioned in 1932, it was attributed to Henry Connelly of Philadelphia. A recent identification of a labeled piece by Connelly resulted in the eager attribution to him of any piece of furniture with stylistic similarities in the legs and feet to his known work.[2] This too-hopeful practice is comparable to the attributions to Phyfe in New York. It has since been determined, however, that the furniture industry in regional centers of federal America was highly specialized by this date and that, for instance, turning shops manufactured legs of a particular design that were distributed as component parts to many different cabinetmaking shops throughout a city.[3] It is, therefore, imprudent to attribute this table, or any undocumented piece, to the workshop most prominently identified with a particular style or detail, although such an attribution seems reasonable.

1. A table once owned by Benjamin Ginsburg and sold at Christie's, New York, Oct. 14, 1983, no. 657, has legs and ornament like the Taft example, but a square top with ovolo corners. Also see Sotheby's, New York, Dec. 8, 1984, no. 290, for a D-shaped console with similar legs and reeded pilasters.

2. See Nancy McClelland, *Duncan Phyfe and the English Regency, 1795–1850,* New York, 1939, p. 226, pl. 213, for a sideboard made for Stephan Girard and attributed to Connelly.

3. Benjamin A. Hewitt, Patricia E. Kane, and Gerald W. R. Ward, *The Work of Many Hands: Card Tables in America, 1790–1820,* exh. cat., Yale University Art Gallery, New Haven, 1982, p. 55.

Provenance Louis Guerineau Myers, New York (sale, American Art Association, Anderson Galleries, Inc., New York, Apr. 7–9, 1932, no. 114); Taft Museum purchase, Apr. 7, 1932.

1932.29

Exhibition New York, American Art Galleries, *Loan Exhibition of Eighteenth- and Early-Nineteenth-Century Furniture and Glass for the Benefit of the National Council of Girl Scouts, Inc.*, Sept. 25–Oct. 9, 1929 (cat. by Louis Guerineau Myers, no. 696).

Literature Nancy McClelland, *Duncan Phyfe and the English Regency, 1795–1850*, New York, 1939, pp. 231, 242, pl. 220; *The Magazine Antiques* (Apr. 1932), p. 182.

1932.2

§●

Possibly by John T. Dolan

Card Table

New York, 1805–10
Mahogany with mahogany and rosewood veneers, with secondary woods of cherry, eastern white pine, and mahogany; H. 73.7 x W. (OPEN) 91.4 x D. 91.4 cm (29 x 36 x 36 in.)

Four fixed legs and a fifth swing, or fly, leg are characteristic of Sheraton-style New York card tables such as this one. Other typical New York features include a double elliptical hinged top and frieze and long, slender, turned and tapered reeded legs beneath plain square capitals and atop attenuated vase-shaped feet. The frieze is veneered with figured mahogany, banded on its bottom edge with rosewood; a panel at its center is likewise defined with rosewood banding. A rosewood quarter-circle is inlaid at each corner of this central panel. The four stiles have narrow cross-banding along the side edges and across the bottom approximately one-half inch above the rosewood banding.[1]

   This card table, attributed to Duncan Phyfe by both Louis Guerineau Myers and Nancy McClelland,[2] is closely related to two card tables of similar form that both bear the label of John T. Dolan, who worked in New York City between 1805 and 1813.

One is in the collection of the Museum of the City of New York, and the other is at Gracie Mansion, the official residence of the mayor of New York City.[3]

1. In 1988, Sotheby's, New York, sold a table virtually identical to the Taft example but having only four legs. See Sotheby's, *Important Americana*, Jan. 28–30, 1988, no. 1895.

2. *The Private Collection of the Late Louis Guerineau Myers*, sale cat., American Art Association, New York, 1932, no. 525; Nancy McClelland, *Duncan Phyfe and the English Regency, 1795–1850*, New York, 1939, p. 160, pl. 129.

3. Benjamin A. Hewitt, Patricia E. Kane, and Gerald W. R. Ward, *The Work of Many Hands: Card Tables in America, 1790–1820*, exh. cat., Yale University Art Gallery, New Haven, 1982, p. 162, ill. p. 163. Also attributed to Dolan by comparison with the two labeled examples are a pair with banded center reserves in the collection at Boscobel (Garrison-on-Hudson, N.Y.); see Berry Tracy, *Federal Furniture and Decorative Arts at Boscobel*, New York, 1981, p. 53, no. 26.

Provenance Louis Guerineau Myers, New York (sale, American Art Association, Anderson Galleries, Inc., New York, Apr. 7–9, 1932, no. 525); Taft Museum purchase, Apr. 9, 1932.

Exhibition New York, American Art Galleries, *Loan Exhibition of Eighteenth- and Early-Nineteenth-Century Furniture and Glass for the Benefit of the National Council of Girl Scouts, Inc.*, Sept. 25–Oct. 9, 1929 (cat. by Louis Guerineau Myers, no. 793).

Literature Nancy McClelland, *Duncan Phyfe and the English Regency, 1795–1850*, New York, 1939, pl. 129.

1932.29

§●

Card Table

New York, 1805–10
Mahogany with mahogany and rosewood veneers, with secondary woods of cherry and eastern white pine; H. 74.9 x W. (open) 91.4 x D. 91.4 cm (29½ x 36 x 36 in.)

This card table, like the one just discussed (see 1932.29), is of standard New York construction with five slender, turned and reeded legs on high vase-shaped feet. The top and conforming frieze, however, are of treble rather than double elliptical shape,

1932.8

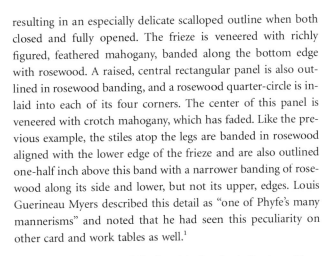

1932.8

1932.7

resulting in an especially delicate scalloped outline when both closed and fully opened. The frieze is veneered with richly figured, feathered mahogany, banded along the bottom edge with rosewood. A raised, central rectangular panel is also outlined in rosewood banding, and a rosewood quarter-circle is inlaid into each of its four corners. The center of this panel is veneered with crotch mahogany, which has faded. Like the previous example, the stiles atop the legs are banded in rosewood aligned with the lower edge of the frieze and are also outlined one-half inch above this band with a narrower banding of rosewood along its side and lower, but not its upper, edges. Louis Guerineau Myers described this detail as "one of Phyfe's many mannerisms" and noted that he had seen this peculiarity on other card and work tables as well.[1]

1. Quoted in *The Private Collection of the Late Louis Guerineau Myers*, sale cat., American Art Association, New York, 1932, no. 303.

Provenance Louis Guerineau Myers, New York (sale, American Art Association, Anderson Galleries, Inc., New York, Apr. 7–9, 1932, no. 303); Taft Museum purchase, Apr. 8, 1932.

1932.8

Card Table

New York, 1805–10
Mahogany and mahogany veneers, with secondary woods of maple and eastern white pine; H. 71.8 x W. 83.8 x D. 43.2 cm (28¼ x 33 x 17 in.)

Closely similar in form and construction to the two preceding examples (see 1932.29 and 1932.8), this table has a double elliptical, or cloverleaf, top, with four stationary legs and one swing

leg. Its distinctions appear in the design of the veneered frieze, which has narrow beading, rather than flat banding, at its bottom edge. Contrasting mahogany veneers create the inlaid geometric patterns of the center panel, which has an interrupted oval within the rectangle, and on the stiles, which have broken, or tombstone, arches.

Provenance Louis Guerineau Myers, New York (sale, American Art Association, Anderson Galleries, Inc., New York, Apr. 7–9, 1932, no. 302 [ill.]); Taft Museum purchase, Apr. 8, 1932.

1932.7

Attributed to Duncan Phyfe

Card Table

New York, 1810–20
Mahogany and mahogany veneers, with secondary woods of cherry and white pine; H. 73.7 x W. 91.4 x D. (closed) 47 cm (29 x 36 x 18½ in.)

The graceful curves and antique associations of the lyre made it a favored motif among interpreters of neoclassical design in the United States. It was frequently adapted in its more literal form as a base for tables of many sorts in Boston and Philadelphia as well as in New York. The Taft lyre-based card table, however, belongs to a much smaller group of tables of New York manufacture in which the far more typical turned balusters are replaced by four sinuous S-scrolls that create an elegantly abstract lyre-shaped support.

The top of the card table operates on a swivel mechanism, a type of construction common to the group. The lower edge of the skirt, which is faced in a contrasting golden mahogany ve-

1932.16

neer, is finished with a beaded edge. The scrolled supports are reeded on their outer faces. This reeding ends well before the supports scroll outward on top. Mounted on the platform base between the four scrolls is a crisply carved pineapple finial sitting atop a spool turning. The platform's face and sides are fluted and support at each corner an inward-curving reeded leg carved with a waterleaf. The legs terminate in brass lion's-paw feet on casters.

In addition to the Taft table, four other examples of related form and construction have been identified, the most similar having a treble elliptical top. It differs, however, in having carved wooden rather than cast-brass paw feet and inlaid satinwood panels rather than fluting on its platform. Like the Taft example, it also has a pineapple finial, although the design differs.[1]

The other known examples of similar card tables are a pair with D-shaped tops and flame finials at Boscobel (Garrison-on-Hudson, N.Y.)[2] and one with a rectangular top with canted corners, owned by the Albany Institute of History and Art.[3] All these tables have been attributed to Duncan Phyfe's workshop. Although no definitive documentation exists for any of them, the extremely high quality of design, workmanship, and materials continues to give strong credence to that attribution.

1. This table, formerly in the collection of Edward Vason Jones, is privately owned.

2. Berry Tracy, *Federal Furniture and Decorative Arts at Boscobel*, New York, 1981, pl. 27.

3. Norman Rice, *New York Furniture before 1840*, Albany, N.Y., 1962, p. 56.

Provenance Louis Guerineau Myers, New York (sale, American Art Association, Anderson Galleries, Inc., New York, Apr. 7–9, 1932, no. 495 [ill.]); Taft Museum purchase, Apr. 9, 1932.

Exhibition New York, American Art Galleries, *Loan Exhibition of Eighteenth- and Early-Nineteenth-Century Furniture and Glass for the Benefit of the National Council of Girl Scouts, Inc.*, Sept. 25–Oct. 9, 1929 (cat. by Louis Guerineau Myers, no. 755).

Literature Nancy McClelland, *Duncan Phyfe and the English Regency, 1795–1850*, New York, 1939, pp. 168–69, pl. 140.

1932.16

❧
Pembroke, or Drop-leaf, Table

New York, 1810–20
Mahogany with mahogany veneers, H. 73.7 x w. 86.4 x
D. (closed) 54 cm (29 x 34 x 21¼ in.)

This small drop-leaf table with one true and one false drawer is of typical New York design and construction. Based on an eighteenth-century form originally attributed to Thomas Chippendale and popularized in the designs of Thomas Sheraton, this simple table is distinguished by its double elliptical leaves, reeded legs with ring turnings, and attenuated vase- and ball-shaped feet. The beading around the drawer is a further refinement.

A table similar to this one now in the Winterthur collection retains the label of George Woodruff,[1] but tables of this quality

1932.16

1932.160

1932.32

and form were certainly made by any number of unidentified makers working in New York during the first quarter of the nineteenth century. They are consistently described in the New York cabinetmakers' price books of that period as Pembroke tables, referring to a design Chippendale is credited with creating for the earl of Pembroke in 1771.[2]

1. Charles F. Montgomery, *American Furniture of the Federal Period*, New York, 1966, p. 351, pl. 331.

2. Berry Tracy, *Federal Furniture and Decorative Arts at Boscobel*, New York, 1981, p. 51.

Provenance [J. P. Zimmerman & Sons, New York]; Taft Museum purchase, June 30, 1932.

1932.160

1932.32

Pembroke, or Drop-leaf, Table

New York, 1810–20
Mahogany with mahogany veneers, with secondary woods of tulip poplar and maple; H. 71.1 x W. (open) 127 x D. 95.8 cm (28 x 50 x 37¾ in.)

Tables such as this one, with turned and carved baluster supports on a rectangular platform that supports four outward-curving legs terminating in claw feet, were a common variation on the form referred to as pillar-and-claw tables during the nineteenth century.[1] This example has a solid mahogany rectangular top with two simple, rounded (or D), hinged leaves. At one end is a drawer with a beaded edge and a stamped brass pull. The opposing end is balanced by a false drawer with matching pull. Pendant finials hang from each stile. The pedestal support consists of four turned balusters with upright waterleaf carving above gadrooned ring turnings. A concave rectangular platform, fluted on its outer sides, supports the four inwardly curving legs, which are carved with waterleafs and reeded. These legs terminate in cast-brass lion's-paw feet atop casters.

The appeal of tables such as these, popular for libraries, parlors, and eating rooms, lay in their versatility, and countless New York workshops produced this form. The surviving examples display numerous variations, some of which have been associated with specific makers. The present example is highly successful in terms of proportion, choice of wood, and quality of carving and is of the type traditionally associated with the workshop of Duncan Phyfe.

1. Berry Tracy, *Federal Furniture and Decorative Arts at Boscobel*, New York, 1981, p. 52.

Provenance Louis Guerineau Myers, New York (sale, American Art Association, Anderson Galleries, Inc., New York, Apr. 7–9, 1932, no. 530); Taft Museum purchase, Apr. 9, 1932.

Literature Nancy McClelland, *Duncan Phyfe and the English Regency, 1795–1850*, New York, 1939, p. 168, ill. p. 148, pl. 127.

1932.32

Pembroke, or Drop-leaf, Table

New York, 1810–20
Mahogany with mahogany and golden mahogany veneers, with secondary woods of white pine and tulip poplar;
H. 72.4 x w. (closed) 96.5 x D. 66 cm (28½ x 38 x 26 in.)

Of typical New York form and construction (see the following entry), this pillar-and-claw drop-leaf table owes its high quality not only to the fine woods chosen but also to the sharpness of its carvings and the strength of its proportions, which together have resulted in its traditional attribution to the workshop of Duncan Phyfe.[1] Its two double elliptical leaves balance its generously wide top and the graceful splay of its curved legs. These legs are carved almost to their ends with well-defined undulating waterleafs, a treatment seen less frequently than shorter waterleafs in combination with reeding. This particular distinction has been associated with the work of Charles-Honoré Lannuier who, along with Duncan Phyfe, was New York's preeminent cabinetmaker during the federal period. However, this table also features a turned-urn pedestal carved with alternating plain and serrated leaves, a characteristic typically associated with Phyfe.[2] Pendant corner drops, a cock-beaded drawer front, and a finely cast brass drawer pull with anthemion motif and foliate back plate are further refinements of this table.

1932.27

1932.27

Contrasting woods appear far less frequently on the late-federal furniture of New York than on that produced in Boston or Philadelphia, and the use of honey-colored veneers on the drawer front and arched panels on the stiles of this table enhances its rarity and appeal. Although obviously a product of one of New York's most skilled cabinetmakers, the table cannot be specifically attributed without further documentation.

1. Louis Guerineau Myers, *Loan Exhibition of Eighteenth- and Early-Nineteenth-Century Furniture and Glass for the Benefit of the National Council of Girl Scouts, Inc.*, exh. cat., American Art Galleries, New York, 1929, no. 760.

2. Edward V. Jones, "Lannuier and Phyfe: Two Creative Geniuses of Federal New York," *American Art Journal*, vol. x, no. 1 (May 1977), pp. 4–14.

Provenance Louis Guerineau Myers, New York (sale, American Art Association, Anderson Galleries, Inc., New York, Apr. 7–9, 1932, no. 516 [ill.]); Taft Museum purchase, Apr. 9, 1932.

Exhibition New York, American Art Galleries, *Loan Exhibition of Eighteenth- and Early-Nineteenth-Century Furniture and Glass for the Benefit of the National Council of Girl Scouts, Inc.*, Sept. 25–Oct. 9, 1929 (cat. by Louis Guerineau Myers, no. 760 [ill.]).

1932.27

Pembroke, or Drop-leaf, Table

New York, 1810–30
Mahogany with mahogany and rosewood veneers,
H. 71.1 x w. (closed) 68.6 x D. 91.4 cm (28 x 27 x 36 in.)

This pillar-and-claw Pembroke table is well proportioned and made of choice, quality mahogany. Its base, an urn pillar, is simply reeded rather than foliate-carved as are two similar examples at Boscobel (Garrison-on-Hudson, N.Y.)[1] and at Winterthur (Del.).[2] Its four reeded legs are carved with waterleafs and are

1932.31

mounted with brass paw feet. The base is attached to the top with a single medial brace. Two double elliptical hinged leaves are supported by a pair of fly leaves on each side. The table has one false and one functioning drawer, each with beaded edges. The lower edge of the apron is cross-banded with rosewood veneer, and a turned pendant drop, suggested by Charles

1932.31

1932.31

Montgomery to be vestiges of the four legs of earlier Pembroke design, hangs from each corner.[3]

Chalked on the underside of the drawer is the signature *Graham.* Whether the name is that of the maker or of a previous owner is uncertain, but it should be noted that in 1805 the New York City directories listed sixty-six cabinetmakers, along with scores of other tradesmen working in such allied fields as carving and turning. Those numbers rapidly increased during the following decades while the style of this table retained its popularity. It is, therefore, impossible without further documentation to attribute a maker or even a more specific date to this fine, yet generic, piece of furniture.

Montgomery described the similar table at Winterthur as being perhaps the most typical furniture form produced in New York during the second decade of the nineteenth century.[4] Extremely practical in size, usually with at least one functioning drawer and always on casters for mobility, Pembrokes such as this one could function equally well as eating, gaming, library, or work tables.

1. Berry Tracy, *Federal Furniture and Decorative Arts at Boscobel*, New York, 1981, p. 52, pl. 35.

2. Charles F. Montgomery, *American Furniture of the Federal Period*, New York, 1966, p. 332.

3. Montgomery, p. 332.

4. Montgomery, p. 332.

Provenance Louis Guerineau Myers, New York (sale, American Art Association, Anderson Galleries, Inc., New York, Apr. 7–9, 1932, no. 529 [ill.]); Taft Museum purchase, Apr. 9, 1932.

1932.31

Classical-Revival Game Table

America, ca. 1830
Mahogany and mahogany veneers with brass inlay, with secondary woods of white pine and cherry; H. 75.6 x W. 91.4 x D. 45.1 cm (29¾ x 36 x 17¾ in.)

An arrangement of brass foliate cutouts and fleurs-de-lis forms a central medallion of vaguely Gothic character inlaid into both sides of the flame mahogany, oblong, hinged leaf of this pedestal-base table. An outline of scalloped, stamped brass banding is inlaid on all four sides of this leaf, and another band of brass ornament combines single- and triple-scalloped and diamond-shaped patterns on its edge. The top, of the same shape as the leaf, is likewise inlaid with the medallion design edged with scalloped brass banding. The frieze beneath it, which accommodates a felt-lined well when the top is swiveled 180 degrees to an open position, has a beaded mahogany edge. On the center, two rounded front corners, and two back corners of the frieze, brass ornaments similar to the ones atop the leaves are connected with a band of interlocking brass circles.

The pedestal base, a massive shaft of turned and carved mahogany, consists of a baluster of clustered acanthus leaves sur-

1.1931

mounted by three rings of foliate gadrooning separated by plain ring turnings. The baluster sits atop two other rings of carved foliage, and the entire ornately carved shaft rests, in turn, on a cylindrical block with carved edges and a brass medallion inlaid on its front face. Four legs with scrolled and carved tops are attached to the block. These legs have flat sides, scroll at the knees, and terminate in fully developed carved paw feet atop brass casters. More brass ornaments are inlaid on their top faces, and they are outlined with inlaid brass stringing along their side edges.

By 1820 American craftsmen had departed from their previous interpretations of classical furniture and replaced the delicate, restrained styles of the early federal period with a weightier, more robust aesthetic. This game table vividly illustrates this

second expression of neoclassicism, often referred to as the American Empire style. It displays an increased emphasis on surface ornament, with both carved wood and inlaid metal embellishment achieving effects of complexity and lavishness.

Furniture inlay of elaborate designs, hand cut from thin sheets of metal and tortoiseshell, found its most rarefied expression during the late seventeenth and early eighteenth centuries in the work of the Frenchman André-Charles Boulle. Ever since, artisans have marveled at that technique. "Boulle," or "Buhl," work, as it came to be known, has enjoyed several revivals and became fashionable during the early nineteenth century in Regency England. Soon it appeared in high-style American furniture as well and was incorporated into the designs of, among others, Charles-Honoré Lannuier and Duncan Phyfe in New York and Joseph Barry in Philadelphia.[1] This type of ornament was also fashionable in Boston at a time when furniture of that city closely emulated English Regency styles.[2]

The Taft table was made about 1830, possibly in New York; the massiveness of the base and the heavy use of gadrooning suggest that city. However, by that date regional distinctions had blurred; without further documentation, attribution to either place of origin or to maker is at best tentative. While neither the quality of the brass inlays nor the carving of this piece is equal to the masterworks produced in Phyfe's or Barry's shops, this table nevertheless is of high quality and was conceived to grace a prosperous Greek-revival parlor. Its mix of neoclassical and Gothic-revival elements marks it as stylistically transitional. Its manufacture is also transitional, utilizing mechanically stamped and rolled metal ornamentation while in the main adhering to traditional handcrafted cabinetmaking techniques.

A table of similar configuration and virtually identical dimensions was sold at Sotheby's, New York, in 1985. That table, made of mahogany and rosewood, has less elaborate brass inlays than the Taft example.[3]

1. See Marilyn Johnson, *Nineteenth-Century America*, New York, 1970, pls. 44 and 71, for examples by Lannuier and Phyfe; and Beatrice Garvan,

1.1931

1.1931

Federal Philadelphia, exh. cat., Philadelphia Museum of Art, 1987, p. 75, for a sideboard by Barry.

2. See Jonathan Fairbanks and Elizabeth Bates, *American Furniture, 1620 to the Present,* New York, 1981, pp. 259–79, for a pair of Grecian couches and a cane-seat *klismos* chair, both in the collection of the Museum of Fine Arts, Boston.

3. Sale, Sotheby's, New York, Jan. 31–Feb. 2, 1985, no. 837.

Provenance Lent by the estates of Louise Taft Semple and Jane Taft Ingalls.

1.1931

❧

Stand or Occasional Table

New York, ca. 1810
Mahogany, H. 72.4 x W. 50.8 x D. 40 cm (28½ x 20 x 15¾ in.)

Small tables or stands with tripod bases and tilt tops were familiar forms throughout the eighteenth century and remained popular across America during the federal period. This example incorporates many of the devices typical of high-style New York

1932.25

1932.25

furniture of the early nineteenth century, including inward-curving legs terminating in brass lion's-paw feet on casters, a vase-and-baluster turned shaft, and an octagonal top. It is crafted of high-quality mahogany. The top of the table is connected to the shaft by means of a mahogany block and brace, in which a brass hinge operates the tilt mechanism.

The table has no carved or inlaid ornament and instead relies on reeding on the face of the legs, ring turning on the vase and baluster, and a beveled, rounded edge on its top to enhance its well-proportioned form.[1]

1. See Sotheby's, New York, *Important American Furniture: The Collection of the Late Berry B. Tracy,* Feb. 1, 1985, no. 763, for a more elaborate example of similar proportions made for Nathaniel Prime and attributed to Charles-Honoré Lannuier.

Provenance Louis Guerineau Myers, New York (sale, American Art Association, Anderson Galleries, Inc., New York, Apr. 7–9, 1932, no. 504); Taft Museum purchase, Apr. 9, 1932.

1932.25

1977.1

§⬥
Dining Table

New York, 1810–20
Mahogany, maple, tulip poplar, and ash; H. 71.1 x w. 266.7
(extending to 411.5) x D. 152.4 cm (28 x 105 to 162 x 60 in.)

Three turned mahogany pedestals, each supporting four splayed legs, form the base of this grandly proportioned dining table. The five individual leaves of the top are joined by sliding brass clamps at both sides. The edges of the leaves are reeded, and the two at the ends have rounded corners. Each leaf is cut from a single board of well-figured, high-quality mahogany, and, when the table is fully extended, the grain of the wood creates a continuous pattern. The pedestal supports are constructed as tapered pillars with ring turnings of the type sometimes referred to as gun-barrel stems. The legs, reeded on their outer faces, terminate in brass paw feet on casters. The three pedestal bases are attached to the three primary leaves by medial braces screwed to the leaves' undersides. The table is illustrated here with three of its five leaves in place.

Dining tables of this type evolved in England during the last quarter of the eighteenth century and are based on the designs of Thomas Sheraton. He wrote in *The Cabinet Dictionary* of 1803:

> The common useful dining-tables are upon pillar and claw, with brass casters. A dining table of this kind may be made to any size, by having a sufficient quantity of pillar and claw parts, for between each of them is a loose flap, fixed by means of iron straps and buttons, so that they are easily taken off and put aside; the beds may be joined to each other with brass fork or strap fastenings.[1]

The obvious advantage to this style was that the center pedestals, with their low, splayed legs, eliminated the awkward seating arrangements made necessary by legs placed at the edges of the tables.

Dining rooms, as such, were uncommon in colonial America. During the federal period, however, they became an inherent part of the architecture of the house. To outfit them, furniture forms including sideboards, servers, and cellarets, as well as large extension tables and sets of chairs, were produced in all the regional cabinetmaking centers.

The Taft dining table was described by Charles O. Cornelius, the New York architect who wrote the pioneering work on Duncan Phyfe,[2] as coming "from a house in Brooklyn where a number of the finest Phyfe examples were found."[3] It was first acquired by Mrs. Harry Horton Bankard, who had herself inherited furniture purchased from Phyfe by her grandmother Mrs. William Minturn[4] and who was an early collector of Phyfe pieces. Mrs. Bankard's collection was sold at the Anderson Galleries in New York on April 20, 1929.

The grand scale, fine quality, and restrained but refined design of this table certainly all suggest the workmanship of Duncan Phyfe. It must, however, be noted that tables similar in type and quality to this one are documented as being made by lesser-known cabinetmakers in both New York City and Albany.[5]

1. Quoted in Christopher Claxton Stevens and Stewart Whittington, *Eighteenth-Century Furniture: The Norman Adams Collection*, Woodbridge, England, 1983, p. 264.

2. See Charles Over Cornelius, *Furniture Masterpieces of Duncan Phyfe*, Garden City, N.Y., 1928, pl. XXXI, for a table similar to this one.

3. Unpublished letter to Walter Siple, May 20, 1932, Taft Museum archives.

4. Nancy McClelland, *Duncan Phyfe and the English Regency, 1795–1850*, New York, 1939, p. 286.

5. See *The Magazine Antiques*, vol. LXXI (June 1957), p. 492, for a table labeled by T. Constantine & Co. of New York offered by John Walton, Inc., and one at Hyde Hall made by John Mead of Albany.

Provenance Mrs. Harry Horton Bankard (sale, Anderson Galleries, New York, Apr. 20, 1929, no. 89 [ill.]); Hulbert Taft, Cincinnati (from Apr. 20, 1929); gift of Mrs. James Benedict (née Katharine Taft), Cincinnati, in memory of her father, Hulbert Taft, 1977.

1977.1

1961.1

Sideboard

Charleston, South Carolina, 1790–1810
Mahogany with mahogany, satinwood, and ebony veneers,
with secondary woods of white pine, red pine, and spruce;
H. 135.3 X W. 212.7 X D. 71.1 cm (53¼ x 83¾ x 28 in.)

Five distinct vertical sections make up the case of this imposing sideboard. The central and largest section is incurving and consists, on top, of a wide flatware drawer divided into three rectangular sections by satinwood string inlay. The middle panel of this drawer is centered with a highly figured satinwood reserve, and the two side panels have string inlay in a horizontal diamond pattern that frames a brass oval-back bale handle with American eagle design. Beneath this central tripartite drawer are two concave doors with large circles of mahogany veneer outlined with satinwood banding defined by ebony stringing.

The other sections of the carcass, two to either side of the central concave plane, are convex, or bow-fronted. The two inner sections protrude the farthest, and the two end sections, although also bowed, recede. Inlay on these four flanking sections repeats the motifs used on the center section—namely, on top, a single horizontal diamond framing a brass pull and, below, a circle. The sections to the immediate left and right of the center are constructed with a single drawer on top and a door below,

whereas the two outside sections, inlaid to give a like appearance of upper drawer and lower door, are actually cupboard doors extending from the top to the bottom of the case.

The stiles adjoining these five sections are inlaid with vertical diamonds on line with the upper drawers and below with narrow panels with ogee arches meeting with a dot at their apex top and bottom. There is a single string of inlay along the entire bottom edge of the case.

Six front and two rear square tapered legs, placed not as much for visual as for structural balance, support the large, undulating carcass. The faces of the front legs are inlaid with an arch-topped tapered panel. Beneath this panel is a one-half-inch cuff of satinwood banding four inches above the floor extending all around the legs. The two rear legs are also cuffed in this manner.

The shaped top of the sideboard is cut from a single mahogany board and is edged with mahogany cross-banding, which extends slightly over the case on all four sides.

The sideboard retains its original tiered wooden gallery, which extends the entire width of the case. It comprises twelve slender mahogany Doric columns, four at each end and four in the midsection supporting a shallow curved shelf. Upon this shelf sits a delicate reticulated railing of ogee-shaped mahogany latticework. Two columns at each of its front and back corners and two others centered on the upper center carcass drawer form the structure for this railing. Between these two center columns is a panel of satinwood framed with mahogany, which repeats the decoration that appears on the drawer beneath. These six upper columns are surmounted by turned mahogany ball finials.

The Taft sideboard is one of a group of four currently identified eight-legged sideboards from the shop of an as-yet-unnamed South Carolina maker. Another one is in the Mabel Brady Garvan Collection at Yale University.[1] The primary differences between it and the Taft example are that the concave center section of the Garvan piece has tambour doors, its eight legs are turned and reeded, and the panel inlaid in its center drawer is engraved with floral decorations. Also, the two inner flanking sections have deep drawers rather than hinged doors beneath their upper drawers. Both of these drawers and the large doors next to them have pull handles centered in their inlaid circles. The Garvan sideboard has a gallery similar to the Taft's, but with squared, rather than rounded, corners, a more elaborately decorated center reserve, and differently shaped finials. Its history is well documented, having descended in the Alston family of Clifton, South Carolina, for five generations.

Another sideboard closely related to the Taft and Garvan examples appears in a photograph of the General William Washington house on South Battery in Charleston.[2] Like the Garvan example, this one has a concave tambour front and turned and reeded legs but does not now have a gallery.

The fourth sideboard of this group offers variations on the previous three. It has the square tapered legs and gallery of the Taft example and the tambour front of the Alston and Washington family ones. This sideboard, which once belonged to the collector and North Carolina resident Alice Kales Hartwick, was sold at auction in November 1989.[3]

In general, American federal sideboards with eight rather than six legs are rare. However, their manufacture was not isolated to one workshop or city, and the dozen or so examples that survive come from several cabinetmaking centers including New York, Hartford, and Baltimore, as well as Charleston.[4] A comparison of these pieces reveals regional idiosyncrasies, and it is apparent that the Taft sideboard is akin to those with South Carolina origins. The use of white and red pine and spruce as secondary woods is appropriate to that area as is the disciplined use of inlay, which is characteristic of Charleston artisans.[5]

The form of the Taft and its related group of sideboards is fully rounded and three-dimensional, relying on its sculptural complexity for impact. The sequence of serpentine curves that creates its profile presents an appearance at once monumental and graceful and a surface both complicated and restrained.

By the 1780s the English designers George Hepplewhite, Thomas Sheraton, and Thomas Shearer had introduced through their design books numerous versions of the sideboard to their interpreters in this country. In the American South simple serving tables, or hunt boards, were popular through the end of the eighteenth century, when advertisements for inlaid sideboards began to appear, and inventories of the period reveal that the sideboard had become a standard feature of dining-room furnishings. Numerous Charleston cabinetmakers, many of them

recent émigrés from Scotland where the form also found favor, are known to have made "elegant commode sideboards."[6] As yet, no maker's name has been associated with any of these four related sideboards.

1. New Haven, Conn., Yale University Art Gallery, Mabel Brady Garvan Collection, inv. no. 1930.2308. See Gerald W. R. Ward, *American Case Furniture in the Mabel Brady Garvan and Other Collections at Yale University*, New Haven, 1988, pp. 428–30 (ill.).

2. See Samuel Chamberlain and Narcissa Chamberlain, *Southern Interiors of Charleston, South Carolina*, Hastings House, N.Y., 1956, p. 110. See also E. Milby Burton, *Charleston Furniture, 1700–1825*, Columbia, S.C., 1955, p. 56, fig. 62.

3. Frank E. Boos Gallery, Bloomfield, Mich., Nov. 4, 1989, no. 251, ill. on cover.

4. See Jonathan Fairbanks and Elizabeth Bates, *American Furniture, 1620 to the Present*, New York, 1981, p. 235, for a spectacular eight-legged sideboard with eglomise panels made in Baltimore. Also see Ward, pp. 420–22, for an example labeled by the New York cabinetmaker James Tabele; and Charles F. Montgomery, *American Furniture of the Federal Period*, New York, 1966, p. 373, for another example believed to be of New York origin. Aaron Chapin of Hartford is also known to have made eight-legged sideboards. See Luke V. Lockwood, *Colonial Furniture in America*, New York, 1913, fig. 207, and James Davidson, *Early American Antiques from the Collection of James Davidson*, exh. cat., Lyman Allyn Art Museum, Boston, 1933, for two examples attributed to Chapin.

5. Burton, p. 56.

6. Burton, p. 55.

Provenance Taft Museum purchase from A. B. Closson, Cincinnati, 1961.

1961.1

Wall Clock

Massachusetts, 1810–20
Mahogany, white pine, gilt gesso, brass, and eglomise, H. 96.5 x W. 26.6 x D. 12 cm (38 x 10½ x 4¾ in.)

This wall clock has a gilt-wood case with applied, twisted gilt roping, which sits atop a concave plinth with composition balls and an acorn pendant. A gilt-wood finial surmounts the face, which is encased in a brass bezel and covered by a convex glass door. Two curved, pierced brackets connect the dial to the lower section. The iron face is painted white with black roman numerals. The hour and minute hands are arrow-shaped. The eglomise panel covering the neck is painted with a swirling feather pattern on a white ground. The lower-case eglomise panel depicts, in polychrome and gilt, Liberty presenting a laurel wreath to the American eagle. This vignette is framed by a foliate border, which is also on a white ground.

In 1802 Simon Willard registered the design of his Patent Improved Timepiece, or what has commonly become known as the banjo clock. The timepiece, with a handmade eight-day movement, is a product of particularly American mechanical and artistic ingenuity. Although always costly, banjo clocks quickly achieved and sustained great popularity, being used

1932.13

tributed a clock, which is very similar to the Taft clock and similarly signed, in the Boscobel collection (Garrison-on-Hudson, N.Y.) to Benjamin Smith, who owned a large clock establishment on the Bowery well into the 1830s.[2]

1. Carl Dreppard, *American Clocks and Clockmakers*, Boston, 1958, p. 274, supp. 42.

2. Berry Tracy, *Federal Furniture and Decorative Arts at Boscobel*, New York, 1981, p. 74, ill. 83.

Provenance Louis Guerineau Myers, New York (sale, American Art Association, Anderson Galleries, Inc., New York, Apr. 7–9, 1932, no. 469 [ill.]); Taft Museum purchase, Apr. 9, 1932.

Exhibition Cincinnati, Music Hall, *The Eagle, An American Decorative Symbol: Cincinnati Antiques Festival Loan Exhibition*, Oct. 17–20, 1991.

Literature Edgar Miller, *American Antique Furniture*, vol. II, Baltimore, 1937, p. 1000.

1932.13

Pair of Wall Brackets

American, ca. 1810
Gilt wood, H. 22.9 cm (9 in.)

These carved and gilded wood brackets are fluted and tapered and terminate in a rounded edge from which hangs a small pendant spherule.[1] A molded shelf with gilt-wood spherules mounted along its front and sides with metal pins surmounts each bracket.

The design of these brackets suggests an enlarged version of many of the bracket bases that form the lower sections of banjo clocks, and it is assumed that they were the product of the same shops that employed the carvers and gilders of these clock cases as well as of mirrors and picture frames.

1. A third wall bracket (1932.6) made up a single lot in the Myers sale with this pair, but it is heavily damaged and does not match this pair.

Provenance Louis Guerineau Myers, New York (sale, American Art Association, Anderson Galleries, Inc., New York, Apr. 7–9, 1932, no. 279); Taft Museum purchase, Apr. 9, 1932.

1932.4, 1932.5

often as wedding gifts or presentation pieces. By 1810 they were being manufactured not only by the Willard family but also by many competing clockmakers, most of them concentrated within the Roxbury section of Boston, and they in turn distributed them to New York outlets.

The Taft clock, which is signed *Smith New York* on the face, is one such Massachusetts "import." The surname Smith appears several times in the directories for New York City clock merchants during the early nineteenth century, including a "B. Smith" and, as of 1810, a "William Smith."[1] Berry Tracy has at-

1932.4, 1932.5

This style of federal looking glass was produced in both New York and Albany during the first decades of the nineteenth century, although this particularly delicate and elaborate example probably dates to the earlier part of the period. Among the numerous gilders, looking-glass makers, and suppliers listed in the directories of this period are J. and J. Del Vecchio and L. Lemut of Albany, and William Wilmerding and John Steen of New York City. The Taft looking glass, however, is unlabeled and cannot be attributed to any particular shop.

1. Similar examples include one in the collection of the New York State Museum, Albany, which also has a view of Mount Vernon on its eglomise tablet but has single columns; and one sold at Christie's, New York, June 16, 1984, no. 276, with a nearly identical frame and eglomise Hudson River scene done in the same manner.

Provenance Louis Guerineau Myers, New York (sale, American Art Association, Anderson Galleries, Inc., New York, Apr. 7–9, 1932, no. 334); Taft Museum purchase, Apr. 8, 1932.

1932.9

1932.9

🐚
Looking Glass

Probably New York City or Albany, 1800–1810
Gilt gesso on pine, with eglomise tablets; H. 109.2 x w. 57.2 cm (43 x 22½ in.)

The gilt-wood frame of this looking glass is composed of two pairs of reeded columns with acanthus-carved capitals, each pair flanking a twisted colonnette. These paired columns support a shaped, molded cornice hung with gilt spherules. Centered on this cornice is a small, gilt-wood, rectangular frame holding an eglomise tablet painted with a stylized compass rose in gilt and black on a white ground. This tablet extends above the cornice and is surmounted by its own cornice and spherules. A gilt-and-grisaille-painted eglomise tablet depicting Mount Vernon surmounts the looking glass.[1]

George Washington's death on December 14, 1799, was commemorated the following spring in New York with the publication of an aquatint reproduction of the artist Alexander Robertson's pastoral drawing of Washington's Virginia home, Mount Vernon. This print soon became one of the most familiar icons of the new republic and is the direct source for the tablet on this looking glass.

🐚
Looking Glass

Probably New York, 1795–1815
Gilt gesso on pine, with eglomise tablet; H. 94.6 x w. 52.7 cm (37¼ x 20¾ in.)

The framework of this looking glass is made up of a series of well-articulated architectural elements rendered in gilt gesso on wood. A molded cornice with various applied ornaments, including twisted roping and, in each cove, a rosette, is supported by a pair of corbels designed as scrolled acanthus foliage. A length of narrow molding forms the bottom edge of this upper section, which frames a horizontal eglomise tablet. This tablet has as its center a pointed elliptical reserve, in which appears a bouquet of a rose and a tulip. This reserve is surrounded by a pattern of chevron stripes alternating with vines and dots painted in black and gold on a white ground. Beneath this tablet, the rectangular looking glass is framed by a pair of fluted columns with Corinthian capitals and rectangular plinths, on which are applied rosettes, like those on the cove above. The bottom rail consists of a strip of simple molding with applied decoration that repeats one of the elements on the cornice molding. This elaborate framework is all applied to a simple nailed pine superstructure.

Looking glasses of this type are based on English Regency prototypes, and most of the plate glass used for them was imported from England or the Continent until well into the nineteenth century.[1] In the United States gilt-wood frames and eglomise tablets were made in the same shops that produced banjo clock cases and picture frames. The Taft looking glass is unlabeled, but its high quality and style suggest either New York or Boston origins.[2]

1. Berry Tracy, *Federal Furniture and Decorative Arts at Boscobel*, New York, 1981, p. 109.
2. Eglomise painting in a freehand style such as appears on this example is traditionally associated with New York. The vine-and-dot motif in

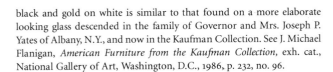

1932.15

1932.3

black and gold on white is similar to that found on a more elaborate looking glass descended in the family of Governor and Mrs. Joseph P. Yates of Albany, N.Y., and now in the Kaufman Collection. See J. Michael Flanigan, *American Furniture from the Kaufman Collection*, exh. cat., National Gallery of Art, Washington, D.C., 1986, p. 232, no. 96.

Provenance Louis Guerineau Myers, New York (sale, American Art Association, Anderson Galleries, Inc., New York, Apr. 7–9, 1932, no. 484); Taft Museum purchase, Apr. 9, 1932.

Exhibition New York, American Art Galleries, *Loan Exhibition of Eighteenth- and Early-Nineteenth-Century Furniture and Glass for the Benefit of the National Council of Girl Scouts, Inc.*, Sept. 25–Oct. 9, 1929 (cat. by Louis Guerineau Myers, no. 740).

1932.15

Looking Glass

Probably Boston, 1812–30
Pine with gilt gesso, with eglomise tablet; H. 78.1 x w. 45.7 cm (30¾ x 18 in.)

This rectangular looking glass is constructed of two concave side moldings with applied twisted roping, a narrow plain bottom molding, and a deeply molded cornice from which hang gilt-wood spherules. Plain rectangular blocks form the capitals that support the cornice at the top, and smaller blocks form the plinths at the bottom. A crosspiece of molding divides the mirrored glass below from the eglomise panel above, which has been painted freehand with a scene of a naval battle framed by a stenciled floral border.

Referred to as a tabernacle glass, the Taft example, which is unlabeled, compares closely with one in the Chipstone collection (Milwaukee, Wisc.) with a painting of a single sailing ship within an acorn-and-oak-leaf border bearing the label *George Dean / Agent in Salem / S. Lothrop's Looking Glass; Manufactory*. Mirrors of this type are associated with both Stillman Lothrop and his brother, Edward Lothrop, who produced them assembly-line fashion in Boston, using mirrored plate glass imported from England. They were then presumably distributed by Dean in Salem throughout the country.[1]

The naval engagement portrayed on the Taft glass took place August 19, 1812, when the U.S. frigate *Constitution* defeated the British frigate *Guerriere* after a half-hour encounter. This and other important battles of the War of 1812 were popular subjects for the eglomise panels on these looking glasses for decades after the event.[2]

1. Oswaldo Rodriguez Rogue, *American Furniture at Chipstone*, Madison, Wisc., 1984, pp. 264–65.

2. See *American Antiques from the Israel Sack Collection*, vol. IV, Washington, D.C., 1974, p. 949, for a different artist's rendering of the

same scene. See also Louis Guerineau Myers, *Loan Exhibition of Eighteenth- and Early-Nineteenth-Century Furniture and Glass for the Benefit of the National Council of Girl Scouts, Inc.,* exh. cat., American Art Galleries, New York, 1929, no. 680, for a scene of Perry's victory; and the New York State Museum, Albany, for an example bearing the label *John Williams 315 Pearl Street NYC,* portraying the encounter between the *Chesapeake* and the *Shannon.*

Provenance Louis Guerineau Myers, New York (sale, American Art Association, Anderson Galleries, Inc., New York, Apr. 7–9, 1932, no. 121); Taft Museum purchase, Apr. 7, 1932.

Exhibition New York, American Art Galleries, *Loan Exhibition of Eighteenth- and Early-Nineteenth-Century Furniture and Glass for the Benefit of the National Council of Girl Scouts, Inc.,* Sept. 25–Oct. 9, 1929 (cat. by Louis Guerineau Myers, no. 697).

1932.3

Toiles de Jouy

Lisa Krieger

1932.217

Jean-Baptiste Huet

Paris 1745–1811 Jouy, France

Jean-Baptiste Huet was the foremost designer and engraver of the French printed cotton textiles known as toiles de Jouy. The son of a court painter, Huet was also trained in decorative arts while in residence at the Louvre. He was equally skilled as an artist and technician and engraved his own cartoons onto the copperplates used in the printing process.

Huet's career at the Oberkampf Manufactory in Jouy, France, spanned more than twenty-five years (1783–1811) and can be defined stylistically into three distinct phases. His earliest work consisted of large-scale picturesque genre scenes printed on a plain ground. Later he connected these asymmetric motifs with a network of delicate scrolls. After 1796 Huet altered his designs significantly to reflect the cultural and political upheavals of post-Revolutionary France. These later works employ neoclassical images rendered on precisely compartmentalized patterned fields.

Huet was the chief designer at the Oberkampf factory until his death in 1811. He left behind a prolifiic repertoire of designs, some of which continued in production until the factory's demise in 1843.

&

Jean-Baptiste Huet, designer and engraver

Leda and the Swan or *Le Lion amoureux*

France, Oberkampf Factory, ca. 1797
Toile de Jouy, copperplate-printed in sepia, on cotton

Rows of rectangular and square reserves, each containing a finely rendered neoclassical motif and bordered with ornamental devices in *le style antique,* are adroitly arranged in this complicated textile design. Identified as both *Leda* and *Le Lion amoureux,* it most prominently illustrates the story of Leda and the swan, along with, in a similarly ornamented mirror-image reserve, that of Androcles and the lion. Between these two familiar allegorical vignettes, a classically draped female figure is flanked by fluted semicircular devices of the sort popularized by the English designers George Richardson and Robert Adam during the mid-1770s.

Among the smaller reserves appear various birds, including owls, eagles, and swans, and animals such as goats, sheep, and hounds. Bird and animal motifs of this type separated from larger scenes featuring human figures originated in Pompeian wall decorations and were revived during the Renaissance by Raphael in his designs for the Loggia at the Vatican. Putti, urns with entwined serpents, winged lions, incense burners, laurel wreaths, and flaming torches are only some of the motifs culled from the vast design vocabulary of the ancient world and translated into the popular culture of the late eighteenth and early nineteenth centuries that appear on this textile. The skillful com-

1932.218

bining of such a wide array of elements into a cohesive design reveals the exceptional talents of Jean-Baptiste Huet.

Although the design of *Leda* is strictly compartmentalized, following the taste of the period, the individual figures, both human and animal, along with the framework, display the depth and sculptural qualities characteristic of Huet's earlier drawing. Also indicative of his skill is the effective use of light, dark, and half-tones that emphasize and clarify the elaborate overall composition. When *Leda* was first printed is unknown, but it was probably introduced during the years 1797–98.

Provenance Elinor Merrell, New York; Taft Museum purchase, 1932.

Exhibition Cincinnati, Taft Museum, *Patterns in a Revolution: French Printed Textiles, 1759–1821*, July 14–Aug. 26, 1990 (cat. by Anita Jones, fig. 11, as *Le Lion amoureux*).

Literature Henri Clouzot, *Histoire de la manufacture de Jouy et la toile imprimée en France*, Paris and Brussels, 1928, pl. 26.

1932.217

Jean-Baptiste Huet, designer and engraver

Les Sphinx médaillons à l'antique

France, Oberkampf Factory, ca. 1805
Toile de Jouy, roller-printed in bister, block-printed in yellow, on cotton

Pairs of sphinxes posed back to back on a fanciful shelf, which balances a roundel enclosing classical figures and a rectangular

reserve framing a musical trophy, are the primary components of this design. Scrolling foliate volutes emanate from the roundel, and swagged vines suspended from pendant finials beneath the shelves connect these elements to female masks at their sides. These masks, in turn, support urn-shaped platforms from which spring hunting dogs in frozen pursuit of birds in flight. From these platforms also spill sheaves of wheat, cattail, and other foliage. Laterally connected to each mask by a ribbon evolving from the headdress are pointed elliptical reserves containing vignettes of kneeling putti presenting doves at a smoking altar. These reserves are surmounted by urns containing loose sprays of laurel leaves and grasses that extend back to the foliage from the smaller urns atop the masks, creating a tracery that connects the various elements of the design. This elaborate network of arabesques is superimposed over a patterned ground of interlocking tripartite arcs, which at their apex contain stylized lotus and iris blossoms.

The design for *Les Sphinx* is included in a collection of drawings by Jean-Baptiste Huet given in 1896 to what is now Le Musée des Arts Décoratifs in Paris.[1] The special skill of that artist for inventively melding eclectic design sources into coherent motifs is well illustrated on this example. Egyptian-revival elements fashionable during the Directoire (1795–99) are freely mixed with Greek, Roman, and Renaissance designs. Yet equally pervasive is the vocabulary of the immediately preceding Louis XVI style—musical trophies, aristocratic sporting dogs, and elegant boughs of grain and foliage. Even the sphinxes themselves, the most overtly Egyptian image, are familiar as eighteenth-century French devices. This eclecticism is to be expected in Huet's work, for although his style evolved throughout his career and was, in fact, radically altered by the Revolution, his artistic sensibilities had been nurtured under the ancien régime.[2] Thus, what appears at first glance to be a purely neoclassical composition reveals itself as reluctant to relinquish the lyrical playfulness of the eighteenth century. In *Les Sphinx* the rational geometry of the framed vignettes is presented in counterpoint to the impossible balance of a superstructure incapable of supporting the compartmentalized reserves.

Huet was a sophisticated artist. He knowledgeably borrowed from the rich library of classical sources at his disposal, including the comte de Caylus's *Recueil d'antiquités supplément*, Raphael's designs for the Loggia at the Vatican, and the engravings of Montfaucon and Piranesi. Yet, while following the latest fashion, he confidently included earlier devices such as swirling baroque foliage and fantastic rococo arabesques. The large scale and the offset register of the repeat are technical devices used by Huet to minimize the static quality of much neoclassical design.

The date *Les Sphinx* was introduced is unknown. The Taft Museum's pieces, which at the time of purchase had survived as a set of nineteenth-century bed hangings, are the only known examples of this pattern. This design can, however, be compared stylistically with others from the Oberkampf factory. *L'Amour vainqueur* (Love Victorious) also incorporates reclining sphinxes, mask heads, and classical scenes in circular, elliptical, and rectangular reserves. That textile has been dated to about 1804.[3] The Taft's textile is printed in two colors— purple-brown and gold, which was a popular combination during the Empire period. This piece also suggests comparison with Huet's *Le Loup et l'agneau* (The Wolf and the Lamb), which likewise has a stacked vertical arrangement with sphinx and mask motifs and is similarly overprinted in yellow, which can be seen in an example now in the collection of the Musée Oberkampf, and which dates from about 1805.[4]

1. Unpublished document no. 9778, dated June 17, 1901, from "les nouvelles collections de l'Union Centrale des Arts Décoratifs."

2. Huet's youth was spent in residence at the Louvre where his father was a court painter, and he continued to live in apartments there until 1801. See Agnes J. Holden, "Jean Baptiste Huet, Master Designer of Toile de Jouy," *The Bulletin of the Needle and Bobbin Club*, vol. XXIII, no. 2 (1939), pp. 9–10.

3. Gilles Pitoiset, *Toiles imprimées: XVIIIe–XIXe siècle*, Paris, 1982, pp. 9–10, pl. 234.

4. Josette Brédif, *Printed French Fabrics: Toiles de Jouy*, New York, 1989, pp. 58–59.

Provenance Elinor Merrell, New York; Taft Museum purchase, 1932.

Exhibition Cincinnati, Taft Museum, *Patterns in a Revolution: French Printed Textiles, 1759–1821*, July 14–Aug. 26, 1990 (cat. by Anita Jones, fig. 13).

Literature *Dessins de J.-B. Huet pour la manufacture de Jouy, 1745–1811*, Les Nouvelles Collections de Musée des Arts Décoratifs au Musée du Louvre, Paris, n.d., ser. 9, pl. 4.

1932.218

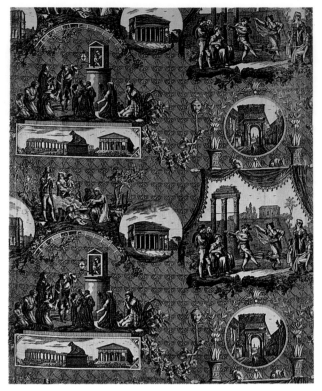

1932.214

Jean-Baptiste Huet, designer and engraver

Le Romain or *Scènes romaines*

France, Oberkampf Factory, ca. 1821
Toile de Jouy, roller-printed in sepia, on cotton
Stamped on selvage: *Manufacture Oberkampf et Widmer aine a Jouy pres Versailles. Bon teint*

The main design element of *Le Romain* (The Roman) is a vignette composed of a pair of dancing figures and a group of onlookers in front of the Temple of Mars Ultor in Rome. The figures in this scene are adapted from a series of engravings entitled *Raccolta di cinquanta costumi pittoreschi* (1809) by the artist Bartolomeo Pinelli.[1] The designer Huet reversed the arrangement of the figures and removed them from their picturesque village setting, placing them instead in front of famous classical Roman monuments. This vignette is framed by a swagged curtain on which sit two naturalistically rendered rabbits and a pair of classical vases. From these vases, sprays of vines rise to frame a roundel, which is centered above this arrangement and encloses a view of the Arch of Drusus. More vines lead from these vases to two mask heads from which, in turn, are suspended swags of grapes. These swags connect to a vignette of worshipers at a roadside shrine to the Virgin and Child. This scene is topped by another view of figures in an encampment atop an arched bridge. To either side are roundels, the one to the left enclosing a view of the Arch of Constantine and the one to the right a view of the Pantheon. Beneath the scene of worshipers is a narrow rectangular framed reserve with a view of the Temple of Neptune and the Basilica at Paestum.

The design is printed on a geometric patterned ground consisting of segmented arcs and semicircles.

The factory mark on the bolt end of this cloth indicates that it was printed after January 1, 1821, when members of the Widmer family, cousins of the Oberkampfs, participated in the reorganization of the financially troubled factory.[2]

1. Josette Brédif, *Printed French Fabrics: Toiles de Jouy,* New York, 1989, pp. 36–37.

2. Henri Clouzot, *Histoire de la manufacture de Jouy et la toile imprimée en France,* Paris and Brussels, 1928, p. 39.

Provenance Edgar Ashley, Foxboro, Mass.; Taft Museum purchase, 1932.

Exhibition Cincinnati, Taft Museum, *Patterns in a Revolution: French Printed Textiles, 1759–1821,* July 14–Aug. 26, 1990 (cat. by Anita Jones, fig. 15).

1932.214

Sheffield Candlesticks

Abby Scher Schwartz

❦
Two Pairs of Candlesticks

England, Sheffield or Birmingham, 1782–1800
Silverplate, H. 34.3 cm (13½ in.)

The wirework standards of these pairs of candlesticks are of the five-stringed lyre form. The urn-shaped sockets are fluted and have reeded edges. The decorative scheme of fluting and reeding is also carried out on the oval, weighted bases. The material with which they are weighted is not original. The candlesticks are unmarked and were electroplated in 1964.[1]

The invention of the process of plating by fusing silver on copper occurred accidentally in 1742 or 1743, when Thomas Boulsover, a Sheffield cutler, was attempting to repair the haft of a knife, part copper and part silver. While soldering, he overheated the metals and discovered that they fused and, more important, that the two metals expanded equally when rolled under pressure.[2] Calling his production "copper rolled plate," Boulsover first manufactured silver-plated buttons and later small boxes and buckles. In 1758 Joseph Hancock, a former apprentice of Boulsover, applied horse- and waterpower to the process, allowing heavier ingots to be rolled into larger plates. The plating process could now be used for large objects formerly the domain of silversmiths: tea- and coffeepots, jugs, saucepans,

1932.11, 1932.12

and candlesticks. Boulsover eventually sold his business to Hancock.[3] Other innovations quickly followed, among them a labor-saving method for constructing multipart candlesticks entirely from cast dies.[4] With the advent of electroplate, an even cheaper though less attractive substitute for solid silver, patented in 1840 by G. R. Elkington, the production of Sheffield plate declined dramatically, so that by 1852 only one workshop in Sheffield was still making Sheffield plate.[5]

Certain technical and stylistic considerations place these pairs of candlesticks between 1782 and 1800. The accuracy and regularity of the fluting and reeding on the bases and sockets indicate that the parts of the candlesticks were made from cast dies, which were introduced in 1765. Plated wirework, used for the lyre-form standards, was the invention of George Whateley, a Birmingham plater who patented his method in 1768.[6] The patent expired in 1782, after which time wirework frequently was used on Sheffield plate wares.[7]

The use of the lyre as a decorative motif was consistent with the neoclassical revival that influenced European taste during the last three decades of the eighteenth century. Its association with antiquity and its elegant lines and graceful curves made the lyre a popular ornamental element in the furniture of Robert Adam in England and Duncan Phyfe in America. During these years, the designers of Sheffield plate reflected current taste and style by incorporating into their wares such classical elements as the lyre, fluting, reeding, acanthus leaf, and shell ornament.[8] After about 1800, the grace and simplicity of design evident in these lyre-form candlesticks began to be replaced by heavier shapes and decorations, reflecting a renewed interest in the opulent rococo with chased and embossed ornament that had characterized the earliest period of Sheffield plate.

1. Most Sheffield plate was unmarked, according to Seymour B. Wyler, *The Book of Sheffield Plate*, New York, 1949, p. 9. According to Wyler, p. 57, bases were filled with rosin and later plaster of Paris. The composition of the existing filling is unknown. The electroplating was done at Cincinnati Plating and Repair Company, according to Taft Museum ledgers.

2. *Oxford Companion to the Decorative Arts*, ed. Harold Osborne, Oxford, 1975, p. 702, s.v. "Sheffield Plate, Old." Sources vary for the discovery date of the process. Henry Newton Veitch, *Sheffield Plate: Its History, Manufacture, and Art*, London, 1908, p. 13, lists 1742, while Arthur Hayden, *Chats on Old Sheffield Plate*, New York, 1921, p. 45, suggests 1743. The entry on Sheffield plate in John Fleming and Hugh Honour, *Dictionary of the Decorative Arts*, New York, 1977, p. 729, places the date of the discovery of the process ca. 1742. Some accounts suggest that the discovery was made when Boulsover used a copper penny in the repair of the knife (Veitch, p. 13), but copper coinage did not exist in England until 1797, according to *The Complete Book of Antiques*, comp. *The Connoisseur*, ed. L. G. G. Ramsey, F.S.A., New York, 1962, p. 1361. This source dates the discovery of the process to 1743.

3. Ramsey, p. 1361.

4. Wyler, p. 56.

5. Fleming and Honour, pp. 729–30.

6. Veitch, p. 65.

7. Ramsey, p. 1407.

8. Sheffield lyre-form candlesticks and candelabra found in the Lowry Dale Kirby Collection of the Colonial Williamsburg Foundation, Winterthur Museum and Gardens, the Gibbons Collection of the Lauren Rogers Museum of Art, and a private collection near Buffalo, N.Y., attest to the popularity of this decorative motif. I am grateful to John D. Davis of Williamsburg and Don Fenimore of Winterthur for bringing these examples to my notice.

Provenance 1932.11 and 1932.12: Louis Guerineau Myers, New York (sale, American Art Association, Anderson Galleries, Inc., New York, Apr. 9, 1932, no. 446); 1932.116 and 1932.117: purchased from Brown's, New York, 1932.

1932.11, 1932.12 and 1932.116, 1932.117

Index of Accession Numbers

Index